growing
plants
indoors

growing plants indoors

j. lee taylor

Michigan State University
East Lansing, Michigan

Illustrations by
Alex Sikkes
Cheryl Anderson
Joseph McCulloch

 Burgess Publishing Company
Minneapolis, Minnesota

Cover design courtesy of Nationwide Papers

Copyright © 1977 by Burgess Publishing Company
Printed in the United States of America
Library of Congress Catalog Card Number 76-56951
ISBN 0-8087-2057-0

0   9   8   7   6   5   4   3   2

Preface

Growing plants indoors has become so popular that there is a shortage of indoor plants. Some of the reasons for the popularity of indoor plants include the concern for the environment, the interest in beautification, the desire to get "back to earth," the large number of hours available for hobbies and recreation, the increasing numbers of retired individuals who want to rekindle their interest in plants, the increasing awareness that working with plants is therapeutic, and finally, the high cost of living, which has created an interest in growing some vegetables and herbs indoors.

This book shows you how to propagate, identify, and care for plants as well as ways to use them in dish gardens, terrariums, and hanging baskets. Most of the plants illustrated can be easily propagated.

Although there are some cultivated varieties (cultivars) included in this manual, most amateurs would do best to learn to identify a greater number of plant species before concentrating on the identification of many cultivars of a single species. This approach will result in the ability to identify, at least by species, the majority of plants handled by florists and garden centers.

I wish to acknowledge the assistance and suggestions given me by Mr. Alex Sikkes, Dr. Everett Emino, Mrs. Cheryl Anderson, and Mr. David Sanford while I was preparing this manual.

Contents

Horticulture and botany

HORTICULTURE

This may be an introduction to plant science for many of you. If you enjoy it as much as other indoor gardeners have, you will hopefully continue to maintain an active interest in plants and go on to study other aspects of horticulture or botany. One of our goals is that you enjoy studying plants at the same time that you learn to grow and work with them.

Even if this is your introduction to one of the plant sciences, you are doubtless aware that both horticulture and botany deal with plants, although you may not be sure of the distinctions between them. The Latin words from which "horticulture" is derived (*hortus* garden and *cultura* cultivation) are a clue to the concerns of this science. Plants grown in gardens are useful to man either for food or for beauty. Although modern horticulture now includes more than "garden cultivation," it still is concerned with cultivated plants having an economic or aesthetic value.

Horticulture is part of the larger field of agriculture. Agriculture is divided into animal and plant sciences. Plant sciences include:

agronomy or *crop science* (the cultivation of field crops, grains, and fibers)

forestry (the production of forest products such as lumber, turpentine, and paper)

horticulture (the cultivation of fruits, vegetables, and ornamental plants)

Horticulture is itself divided into four traditional subject areas:

pomology (fruits)

olericulture (vegetables)

1

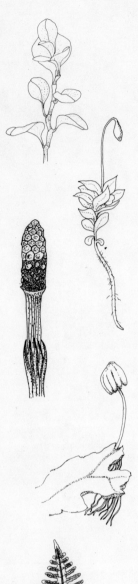

ornamental horticulture (trees, shrubs, turf grasses, and ground covers)

floriculture (flowers and small ornamental plants)

Indoor plants are a part of floriculture.

BOTANY

Horticulture is an applied science. Its counterpart is the pure science of botany. Botany is concerned with the study of non-cultivated (wild) plants. There are many subject areas within this field. Some of the more important ones include:

anatomy (study of the detailed structure of plants)

ecology (study of the relationships between organisms and their environment)

genetics (study of heredity)

morphology (study of the form and structure of plants)

paleobotany (study of fossil plants)

pathology (study of plant diseases)

physiology (study of the processes and functions of plants and plant parts)

taxonomy (study of plant identification and classification)

A sound background in botany is a great asset to the horticulturist as he works with plants.

PARTS OF A PLANT

All commonly grown plants are composed of the same basic parts—roots, stems, and leaves. These three parts are present throughout the entire life of the plant. In addition, most mature plants will produce reproductive structures if environmental conditions are suitable. The most familiar reproductive structures are flowers and cones.

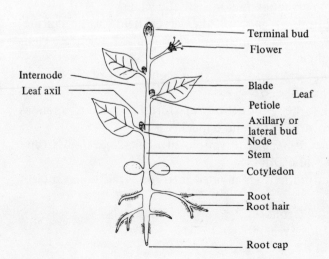

Roots

Function and Growth. Roots are one of the three vegetative organs of plants. They usually grow underground where they serve to anchor the plant and absorb water and nutrients from the soil or growing medium. A third function of many, but not all, roots is the storage of food. Carrots, beets, and turnips have edible fleshy storage roots. A major difference between roots and stems is that roots do not have nodes and internodes.

Anchorage

A closer look at roots shows that they consist of four main regions: root cap, meristem, area of cell elongation, and area of cell differentiation. Near the tip of every root is a region of very small, dense cells. This is the *meristem,* where a small group of constantly dividing cells adds new cells onto the root. As the growing root tip is pushed through the soil, these delicate meristematic cells are protected by the *root cap*. The outer cells of the root cap are sloughed off by abrasion with soil particles, but they are replaced with new cells produced by the meristem.

Just behind the meristem is a region characterized by the *elongation* of newly formed cells. The force exerted by these elongating cells is what pushes the root tip downward through the soil.

Absorption

Above the zone of cell elongation is an area where the cells begin to take on different appearances and functions. This is the area of *cell differentiation*. It is also characterized by the appearance of root hairs which are slender extensions of the surface cells. Root hairs increase the surface area of the root so that it can absorb water and nutrients more efficiently.

Cells stop elongating in the region of the root hairs. If they continued to push the root through the soil in this area,

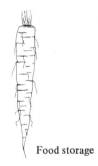

Food storage

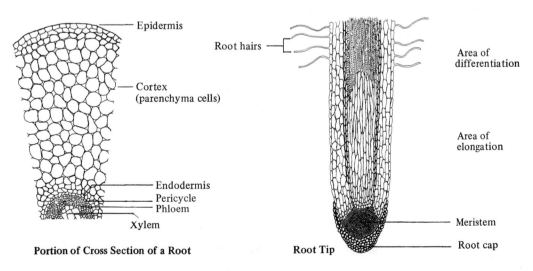

Epidermis

Cortex (parenchyma cells)

Endodermis
Pericycle
Phloem
Xylem

Portion of Cross Section of a Root

Root hairs

Area of differentiation

Area of elongation

Meristem

Root cap

Root Tip

4

the root hairs would be torn off because they are held in place by soil particles.

Root hairs grow only in a narrow region near the root tip. But because there are many root tips, a plant usually has many root hairs. The life of each root hair is only several days or weeks. Old root hairs die, but they are replaced by new ones so that the total number remains about the same.

It is very important to preserve as many root hairs as possible when transplanting a plant, since loss of root hairs greatly reduces the water-and-nutrient-absorbing surface area of the roots. Unfortunately, root hairs are closely entwined around soil particles and are easily pulled off if not enough soil is removed during transplanting or if the plant is handled roughly. Root hairs die quickly when exposed to air, which is another reason for keeping a sufficiently large ball of soil around the plant. Watering the soil before transplanting helps the soil particles adhere to each other and to the root hairs.

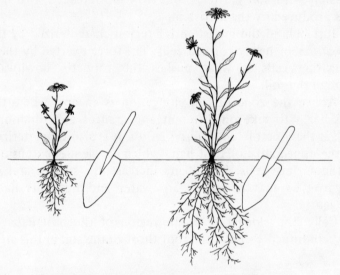

Small plants with less extensive root systems can usually be transplanted with more success than large plants.

Some plants are able to regenerate lost root hairs more easily than others, and so are more likely to withstand the shock of transplanting. Also, small plants are more likely to be successfully moved than large plants that have more extensive root systems. Misting, shading, or cutting back the transplanted plant may help reduce water loss from the leaves until the roots recover their full water-absorbing capacity.

For the most part, roots grow in a downward direction. There is some lateral growth, but sooner or later the root tips turn downward. This is a hormone-regulated response to gravity, called *geotropism*, which will be discussed later.

Roots appear to grow towards water, but this is not really true. Actually, vigorous root development is promoted where roots encounter optimum moisture levels and retarded where they encounter soil that is too wet or too dry.

Types of Roots. When you look at a plant, you are really seeing only half of it. The other half (probably just as large as the part you see) is underground. Few people are familiar with entire root systems because we hardly ever see all the roots exposed at the same time.

Even so, various types of roots have been identified and you will probably recognize most of them. The first root of a new plant that emerges out of a germinating seed is called the *primary root*. The primary root usually gives rise to a series of branches that are called *secondary roots*. In many plants the secondary roots grow faster than the primary root and become the whole root system. Sometimes, however, the primary root remains dominant. This is true of the carrot, in which the thick fleshy part is the primary root.

Sometimes the primary and secondary roots fail to grow and are replaced by new roots that grow out of the stem. This is what happens in many grasses. The new roots are called *adventitious* roots. This term also applies to any roots that arise from some structure other than a primary or a secondary root. Adventitious roots are very common. All the roots that develop on stem or leaf cuttings are adventitious, as are roots that develop at the nodes of certain ivies, or roots that grow from bulbs and corms.

Primary, secondary, and adventitious are terms used to classify roots and other plant organs according to *origin*. Roots can also be classified according to the kind of root *system* they form. There are two main types of root systems. One is the *taproot* system, in which the primary root remains the largest root and all of the secondary roots are smaller. The taproot can be slender, fleshy, or woody. Familiar examples are carrots, radishes, and Queen Anne's lace.

The other main system is the *fibrous* or *diffuse* root system, which all grasses and most garden and houseplants have. A fibrous root system has many slender roots, the main branches of which are all nearly equal in size. Fibrous roots may be secondary or adventitious in origin. Sweet potato, dahlia, and tuberous begonia have a fibrous root system in which the larger roots become enlarged with stored food. These enlarged roots are usually referred to as *tuberous roots* and may be adventitious (sweet potato and dahlia) or primary (begonia).

The *aerial* roots of *epiphytes* like bromeliads and orchids are specialized roots which help anchor the plant to a tree rather than to the ground. Epiphytes are plants that live

Fibrous root system

Taproot

Aerial roots of orchid

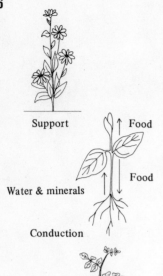

Support

Water & minerals

Conduction

Food

Food

Food storage

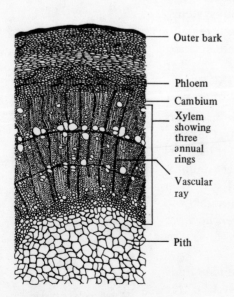

Cross-section of trunk
of 18-year-old tree

perched non-parasitically on other plants. The aerial roots of epiphytic orchids like cattleya are quite unusual; they are able to absorb water from the atmosphere.

Stems

Functions and Growth. Stems of flowering plants have several functions. First, they produce and support leaves, flowers, and fruits. Second, they conduct water and minerals from roots to leaves, and food from leaves to other parts of the plant, including roots. Water, food, and minerals travel through a system of tubes that make up the vascular or conducting tissue of the plant. A third function of some stems is food storage. The Irish potato is an underground stem that stores food.

Stems, like roots, characteristically increase in length only near the tip. If you carve your initials in the bark of a tree and return 20 years later, they will be at the same height that you originally carved them. The reason for this is that the tree does not lengthen at the base, but only at the tip. Trees do, however, increase in diameter all along the trunk; each year a new layer of wood is formed. This can be seen in the annual rings of a tree trunk that has been cut through. Since the base of the tree is the oldest part, it has more annual rings that the upper sections do.

Trees are plants that have a hard, woody stem which increases in diameter each year. A tree normally has just one main stem or trunk that rises some distance above the ground before it branches. Most shrubs have numerous woody stems which usually branch just above the soil line.

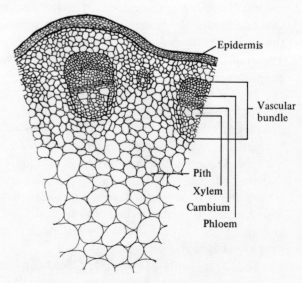

Outer bark

Phloem

Cambium

Xylem showing three annual rings

Vascular ray

Pith

Epidermis

Vascular bundle

Pith

Xylem

Cambium

Phloem

Portion of Cross Section of a Woody Stem

Portion of Cross Section of an Herbaceous Dicotyledonous Stem

Trees and shrubs normally live for many years and are *perennials*. A perennial is a plant that lives several to many years, producing both leaves and flowers each growing season after it has reached maturity. Not all perennials are woody. Some perennials, such as peonies and shasta daisies, have soft, green, herbaceous stems that die back at the end of each growing season. Hardy underground structures enable these *herbaceous perennials* to survive winter and live for many years.

Many herbaceous plants live for only one growing season. At the beginning of the season they grow rapidly and produce flowers and seeds, and then die. Such plants are called *annuals*. Many garden flowers such as marigolds, zinnias, and petunias are annuals.

Some plants live for 2 years and are called *biennials*. They produce only stems and leaves the first year. The second year they flower, set seeds, and die. Examples are beets, carrots, hollyhocks, snapdragons, and pansies. Some biennials such as snapdragons and pansies are treated as annuals, since they are usually purchased in the spring of the year that they will flower.

Herbaceous stems are soft and green with relatively little growth in diameter. Plants having herbaceous stems may be annuals, biennials, or perennials. Woody stems are hard and brown, and increase in diameter each year. Nearly all plants having woody stems are perennials.

Kinds of Stems. Most plants have *aerial* stems, which are stems that grow above the soil. Many plants have *erect* stems that are either herbaceous or woody as previously described. Some plants like grape and morning glory have *climbing* stems. In other plants such as watermelon and squash, the stems are *prostrate* or creeping.

Tree

Shrub

Erect stem

Climbing stem

Underground stem: lily bulb

Prostrate stem

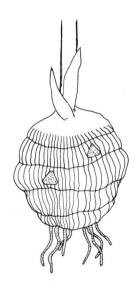

Underground stem: gladiolus corm

8

ANNALS, BIENNIALS, AND PERENNIALS
IN SUMMER AND WINTER

	Summer	Winter	Summer	Winter	Summer	Winter
Annuals						
Biennials						
Herbaceous Perennials						
Perennials						

Leaves

Function. Leaves can be regarded as flattened and expanded parts of the stem. Their function is to convert light energy into chemical energy by manufacturing simple sugar from carbon dioxide and water in the presence of sunlight and chlorophyll (the green pigment in plants). This process, called *photosynthesis*, will be discussed later. Although leaves may be highly *modified* (changed), the thin broad surfaces of ordinary foliage leaves greatly increase the plant's surface area for efficient interception of sunlight.

Growth. Roots and stems follow a pattern of *indeterminate* growth—they continue to grow at the tip as long as the plant is alive. Leaves, however, exhibit *determinate* growth. They soon reach a maximum size, then mature and function for one or many seasons. Stems terminating in a flower bud also exhibit determinate growth.

Terms. Most leaves consist of a *leaf stalk* called the *petiole* and a flattened, expanded portion at the end of the petiole called the *blade.* The leaves of some plants, like tradescantias, have no petioles but have the leaf blade attached directly to the stem. This type of leaf attachment is termed *sessile.* A few plants have *perfoliate* leaves, where the base of each leaf extends around the stem.

The place where leaves or buds originate on a stem is termed a *node.* The space between two adjacent nodes is

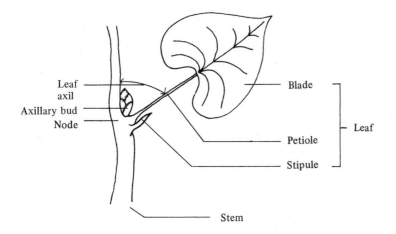

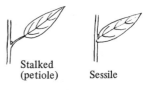

Stalked
(petiole)   Sessile

Perfoliate

Leaf Attachments

called an *internode,* and it varies in length from very short to very long. The angle between the leaf and stem is called the *axil.* The bud located at this juncture is called an *axillary bud* or *lateral bud* to distinguish it from the *terminal bud* at the growing tip. Some plants also have leafy or scaly structures at the base of a petiole called *stipules.* Stipules may be large and green like a leaf, or they may be modified into spines or tendrils. Stipules, when present, are considered to be part of the leaf.

Leaf Arrangement. The arrangement of leaves on a stem is important in plant identification. The four most common types are *alternate, opposite, whorled,* and *basal rosette.*

Alternate: one leaf at a node

Opposite: two leaves at a node opposite each other

Whorled: three or more leaves at a node

Basal Rosette: leaves clustered together close to the ground

Opposite   Alternate

Whorled   Basal rosette

Leaf Arrangements

Leaf Venation. Veins or vascular strands occur in three basic patterns in leaf blades: *parallel, palmate,* and *pinnate.*

Parallel venation: veins extend from the base to the tip of the blade, or extend from the mid-vein to the edge of the blade parallel to each other.

Palmate venation: veins form a web or net between three or more main veins which spread out from the base of the blade.

Pinnate venation: one central vein runs the entire length of the blade and many secondary veins form a web or net.

Leaf Structure. A cross section of a leaf as seen under a microscope would show three main tissues: *epidermis,* the layer of cells comprising the upper and lower leaf surfaces; *mesophyll,* the central portion of the leaf, made up of two different areas; and veins or vascular bundles, consisting

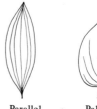

Parallel   Palmate

Pinnate

Venation Patterns

mainly of *xylem* cells which conduct water and nutrients upward and *phloem* cells which conduct food downward. The epidermis helps protect the central portion of the leaf from drying out, and often the epidermal cells secrete a waxy waterproof substance (*cutin*) which forms a layer (*cuticle*) over both leaf surfaces. *Stomates* or *stomata* are also located in the epidermis layer and consist of two *guard cells* and a small opening (*stoma*). The guard cells control the opening and closing of the stoma.

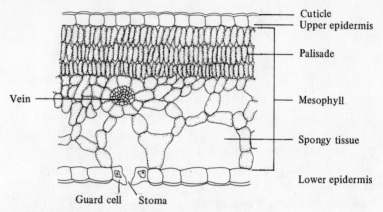

Kinds of Leaves. There is much variation among leaves. Some highly modified leaves may be reduced to mere scales which soon fall off, as in some cacti, or they may be as elaborate as the insect-trapping structures of the insectivorous plants. Even ordinary leaves differ greatly in size, shape, coloration, type of *margin* (boundary area on edge), thickness, and presence or absence of hairs.

A leaf that has an undivided blade (although the margin may be deeply indented) is called a *simple* leaf. If the blade is divided into separate parts (*leaflets*), it is *compound*. Com-

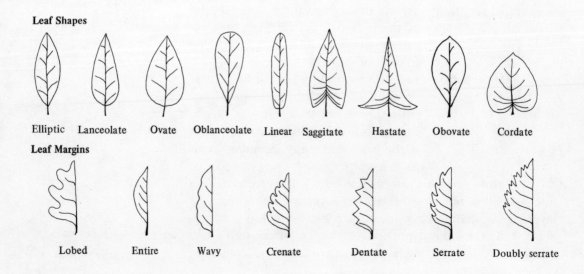

pound leaves may be pinnate or palmate depending on whether the leaflets arise along the sides of a central petiole (*rachis*) or fan out from the tip of the petiole. The stalks of leaflets are called *petiolules*. It is sometimes difficult to distinguish a simple leaf from a leaflet. One clue is to look for the axillary bud; simple leaves will have one at the base of the petiole, but leaflets will not.

Flowers and Fruits

Function and Structure. Although many plants reproduce *asexually* (vegetatively), sexual reproduction is important for most plants. The flower is the part of the plant that contains its reproductive organs. Not all plants have flowers and seeds. Molds, mosses, and ferns reproduce by means of single-celled bodies called spores. Pines, spruces, and many other gymnosperms have cones instead of flowers, but all of these groups show sexual reproduction.

A flower is really a special kind of branch whose leaves have become crowded together and modified into the various flower parts. Most flowers are made up of four different parts or floral organs. Outermost are the *sepals*. Sepals are often green and leaf-like, and their function is to protect the other floral parts in the bud stage. The sepals are collectively called the *calyx*. The most conspicuous floral part is found just inside of the sepals. These are the *petals*, which are often colored and serve to attract insects. Flowers that do not rely on insects to pollinate them often have insignificant petals or even none. The complete ring of petals in the flower is called the *corolla*. The calyx and corolla together are known as the *perianth*.

Toward the center from the perianth are the male floral parts, called *stamens*. Usually a stamen consists of a stalk-like

11

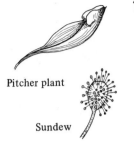

Pitcher plant

Sundew

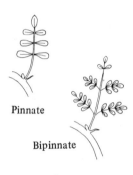

Venus' flytrap

**Highly Modified Leaves of
Insectivorous Plants**

Pinnate

Bipinnate

Palmate

Compound Leaves

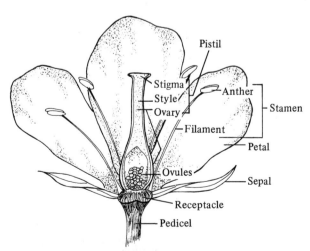

Section of a Flower

(labels: Pistil, Stigma, Style, Ovary, Anther, Stamen, Filament, Petal, Ovules, Sepal, Receptacle, Pedicel)

12

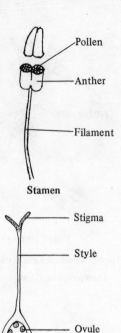

Pollen

Anther

Filament

Stamen

Stigma

Style

Ovule

Ovary

Pistil

Complete flower

Incomplete but
perfect flower

portion called the *filament* and a box-like part called the *anther*, in which *pollen* is produced. Pollen contains the male sex cells which are necessary for fertilization.

In the center of the flower are found one or more *pistils*. The pistil is the female part of the flower, which will later become the fruit and bear the seeds. The pistil usually has three parts. At the top is the *stigma*, the purpose of which is to catch pollen. To accomplish this, the stigma is often sticky. At the bottom of the pistil is the swollen part called the *ovary*, which contains the *ovules* that eventually become the seeds. The part between the stigma and ovary is called the *style*. All the flower parts are attached to the somewhat swollen tip of the flower stalk (*pedicel*), which is called the *receptacle*.

A flower that has all four sets of organs (sepals, petals, stamens, and one or more pistils) is known as a *complete* flower. When a flower lacks one or more of these parts it is said to be an *incomplete* flower. A flower that contains both sex organs (stamens and one or more pistils) is known as a *perfect* flower. If a flower contains only stamens or only pistils, it is called an *imperfect* flower. Imperfect flowers are referred to as being either staminate (male) or pistillate (female) depending on which sex organs are present. A *monoecious* plant has both male and female flowers on the same plant. Corn is a familiar example: the tassel is made up of male flowers and the ear consists of female flowers. The silks that emerge from the end of the ear are actually stigmas which catch the wind-borne pollen.

A few plants are *dioecious*, which means that male and female flowers are produced on separate plants. Holly is a dioecious plant. In order to obtain red berries on the female plant, a male plant must be planted nearby.

Flowers that can be divided into equal halves by any cut through the center are said to have *radial symmetry* (chrysanthemum, lily). Flowers having *bilateral symmetry* can be divided into equal halves by only a single cut through the center (orchid). Flowers having *irregular symmetry* cannot be divided into equal halves (canna).

Incomplete and imperfect flower

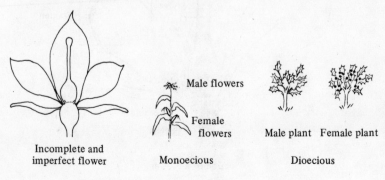

Incomplete and imperfect flower

Male flowers

Female flowers

Monoecious

Male plant Female plant

Dioecious

Flower structure itself can vary greatly—many parts can be greatly modified or missing entirely. Non-floral organs such as *bracts* may imitate petals. The red "petals" of the poinsettia are really bracts; the real poinsettia flowers are found within the greenish-yellow structures at the center. Sometimes the floral organs themselves have undergone changes. Sepals and stamens may look like petals. The six "petals" of an Easter lily are actually three petals and three sepals that all look alike. The extra petals of double roses were once stamens.

Many plants have single flowers, each at the tip of a flower stalk. Often, however, flowers are grouped together and are attached to the same stalk. Such a flower cluster is called an *inflorescence*. Inflorescences are differentiated on the basis of how the flowers are attached to the stalk and on their order of opening. In the accompanying diagram, the largest circles represent flowers that open first and smaller circles represent those that open later. The stalk supporting the inflorescence is called the *peduncle* and the stalks of individual flowers are called *pedicels*.

Fruit and Seed Formation. The steps involved in fruit and seed formation are: formation of sex cells or *gametes* (egg and sperm); pollination; fertilization; and ovary and ovule maturation. Ovules are the egg-containing organs located inside the ovary. Each ovary may contain one or more ovules. Pollen is produced in *anthers*, which open and release pollen grains when they are mature. These grains contain sperm which function during the fertilization.

The beginning of fruit and seed formation occurs when pollen from an anther is transferred to the stigma of a pistil. This process is called *pollination*, and it may be accomplished by insects, wind, or birds. Once on the stigma, pollen grains germinate and a *pollen tube* from each grain starts to grow down through the style and ovary into an ovule.

Fertilization occurs when a sperm nucleus from the pollen tube unites with the egg nucleus inside an ovule. The fertilized egg develops into an *embryo* and the ovule develops into a seed. The ovary develops into a fruit containing one or more seeds.

There are many different types of fruits. Common examples are: *berry* (tomato), *pepo* (cucumber), *drupe* (cherry), *pome* (apple), *achene* (sunflower), *nut* (oak), *legume* (pea), *capsule* (snapdragon), *aggregate* (raspberry), and *multiple* (pineapple).

Seeds. A plant seed is really a very young plant which has not yet begun to grow actively but which is very much alive. This miniature plant (embryo) is protected by a seed coat which surrounds it. The seed coat is usually a tough water-

Radial symmetry

Bilateral symmetry

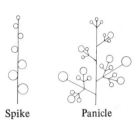

Spike   Panicle

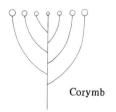

Head   Raceme

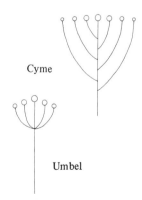

Corymb

Cyme

Umbel

Kinds of Inflorescences

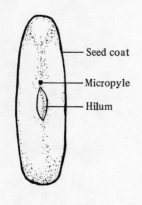

Seed coat

Micropyle

Hilum

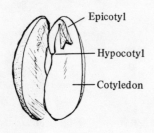

Epicotyl

Hypocotyl

Cotyledon

proof covering that protects the embryo from drying out, mechanical injury, and insect and disease damage.

Seeds come in many different sizes, shapes, and colors. Most of them have the following basic parts:

1. The seed coat or protective covering.
2. The embryo itself. It has three parts:
   a. *Cotyledon*(s)—the part of the embryo that stores and digests food for the young plant.
   b. *Epicotyl*—the part that becomes the stem, located above where cotyledons are attached.
   c. *Hypocotyl*—the part of the embryo which will become the first root of the seedling (a young plant grown from a seed), located below where the cotyledons are attached.
3. The *endosperm.* This is food-storing tissue. Some embryos use it up before the seed is mature, so the seed has no endosperm when it is planted. Seeds of beans, peas, and pumpkins contain no endosperm, because the embryo has used it up. These plants have food stored in the cotyledons.

PLANT TAXONOMY

Plant taxonomy is concerned with the identification, naming, and classifying of plants. Before discussing a particular plant's characteristics, culture, and method of propagation, it is desirable to be able to identify and name the plant in question. Knowing the relationship of one plant to another plant may also be beneficial when comparing plant parts, growth habits, and methods of propagation.

Classification of Plants

Several plant classification systems are in use today. The basis of plant classification is primarily the reproductive structures, with vegetative characters being of lesser importance. This is because reproductive structures are usually more stable and less subject to the effects of environmental factors than are the vegetative plant parts. The relationships of plants are another important basis for classification.

The plant kingdom is usually broken down into two main groups or subkingdoms. They are:

Subkingdom *Thallophyta* (plants not forming embryos, such as algae, bacteria, and fungi)

Subkingdom *Embryophyta* (plants forming embryos, such as mosses, pines, and coleus)

Each subkingdom is divided into smaller taxonomical units called *phyla* (plural of *phylum*). Thus, the phyla included in the subkingdom *Embryophyta* are:

Phylum *Bryophyta* (plants lacking vascular tissues, such as mosses and liverworts)

Phylum *Tracheophyta* (plants having vascular tissue)

Each phylum is divided into smaller units (*subphyla*) such as in phylum *Tracheophyta*:

Subphylum *Sphenopsida* (horsetails)

Subphylum *Pteropsida* (ferns and seed plants)

The subphylum *Pteropsida* is broken down into smaller units called classes:

Class *Filicineae* (ferns)

Class *Gymnospermae* (plants having naked seeds, usually in cones)

Class *Angiospermae* (plants having covered seeds; the true flowering plants)

The class *Angiospermae* is divided into subclasses:

Subclass *Dicotyledonae* (flowering plants with two cotyledons in the embryo and flower parts usually in fours or fives)

Subclass *Monocotyledonae* (flowering plants having one cotyledon in the embryo and flower parts usually in threes)

Successively smaller taxonomic units below the subclass are order, family, genus, and species. Classification systems vary mainly with the major groupings of plants and not at the family level and below.

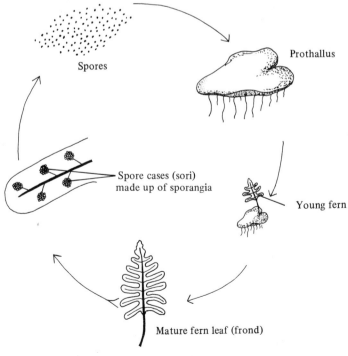

Fern Life Cycle

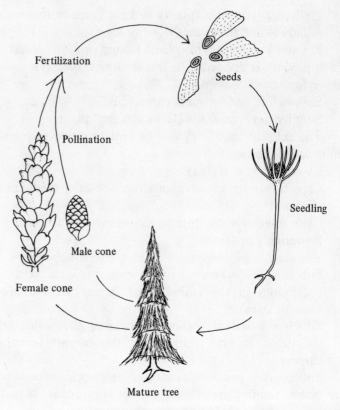

Fertilization

Pollination

Seeds

Seedling

Male cone

Female cone

Mature tree

Gymnosperm Life Cycle

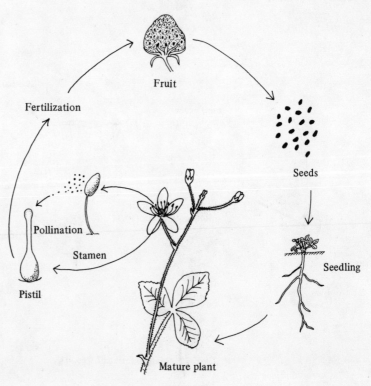

Fruit

Fertilization

Pollination

Stamen

Seeds

Pistil

Seedling

Mature plant

Angiosperm Life Cycle

Dicots and Monocots. Angiosperms (the true flowering plants) are divided into the two subclasses Dicotyledonae and Monocotyledonae, commonly referred to as dicots and monocots. Differences in flower structure are one basis for this classification. This points out the importance of flowers as a criterion in plant classification.

Monocots get their name from the fact that their seedlings have only one cotyledon. A *cotyledon*, or seed leaf, often stores food for the embryo and young plant. It may be one of the first green structures to appear above ground when a seed germinates, although some cotyledons remain below ground. It is not a true leaf and does not persist, but dries up as food is withdrawn from it.

Monocots are also differentiated on the basis of their leaves and flowers. The leaves are parallel veined and they rarely have petioles. The flower parts are present in units of three or multiples of three such as three sepals, three petals, and three stamens. The sepals may look just like the petals, as in lilies and tulips. Monocots include such plants as lilies, irises, palms, orchids, and grasses.

The seedlings of dicots always have two cotyledons. Most Angiosperms are dicots. Dicots usually have net-veined leaves and flowers with parts in units and multiples of four and five. Most common garden flowers, wildflowers, trees, fruits, and vegetables are dicots.

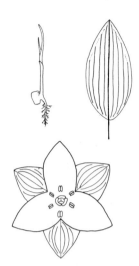

Monocots

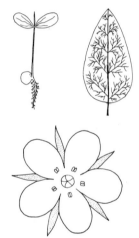

Dicots

Naming Plants

Common Names. Plants have come to be known by common names like beech, ladyslipper, and maidenhair fern. Though easy to remember, common names can make it hard to talk about a specific plant. Many plants have more than one common name: marsh marigold = cowslip; trillium = wake-robin; dogtooth violet = trout lily = adder's tongue;

Dog-tooth violet

Trout lily

Adder's tongue

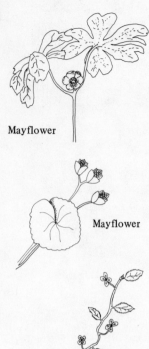

Mayflower

Mayflower

Mayflower

Felis domesticus

Ananas comosus

*Chrysanthemum
leucanthemum*

Rattus rattus

strawberry begonia = strawberry geranium. Sometimes the same name is used for different plants (at least six plants in the world are known as mayflower). Now you can see why common names are often confusing.

Scientific Names. A more precise way of naming plants was established in the eighteenth century by Carolus Linnaeus. It involves the use of a *binomial nomenclature* for plants and animals. This means that each plant is given one name (the scientific name) consisting of *two parts*. The first part is a noun and is the name of the *genus* to which the plant belongs. The second word is an adjective and is the name of the plant's *species*. Scientific names are always in Latin, always written in italics (or underlined), and the first letter of the generic name is capitalized while the name of the species remains in lower case. Sometimes an initial, abbreviation, or name follows a scientific name and indicates who named that particular species. Thus, *Mimosa pudica*, L. was named by Linnaeus and is the common "sensitive plant."

The International Code of Botanical Nomenclature sets up the rules for naming plants and insures that every plant has only one scientific name that is accepted by scientists all over the world. Although most people do not know the scientific names of the plants they grow, it would be desirable to have a reference book that does give scientific names. A reference book is especially handy when you are purchasing plants. Even houseplants are known by different common names, and to insure that you are getting what you want, it is helpful to check the scientific name.

Family, Genus, Species. A family is a group of similar genera that are thought to be related to each other. Members of the same family resemble each other more than they do members of another family. African violets, episcias, gloxinias, and streptocarpus all belong to the same family, the Gesneriaceae family. They are all tropical plants having showy flowers of similar structure, and opposite or basal leaves.

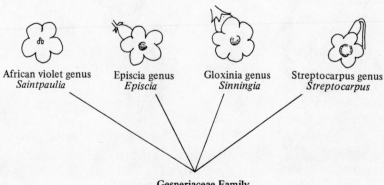

African violet genus
Saintpaulia

Episcia genus
Episcia

Gloxinia genus
Sinningia

Streptocarpus genus
Streptocarpus

Gesneriaceae Family

Plants in this book are grouped into families and some characteristics of each family are given. If you look for family characteristics when you learn the plants, it may help you understand how they are related and may even help you identify them.

The next smallest group to which a plant belongs is the *genus*. A genus (plural = genera) is a group of similar species that are thought to be related to each other. Species that belong to the same genus resemble each other more than they do species of another genus. *Sinningia pusilla* is a tiny plant (2 inches high) that is sometimes grown in terrariums. As you can see by the generic name, *Sinningia*, it is related to gloxinias (*Sinningia speciosa*), and you would expect its flowers to resemble gloxinias because they belong to the same genus.

Sinningia pusilla

The smallest natural group to which a plant belongs is the *species*. A plant species is the smallest group of individuals that are more like each other than they are like any other kind of plant and that maintain their individuality through successive generations. In other words, a species is just *one* kind of plant, like the gloxinia. Gloxinias have large trumpet-shaped flowers that are available in pure or mottled tones of red, purple, or white. Even though different gloxinia plants have flowers of different colors, they are still more like each other than they are like any other kind of plant. If you plant gloxinia seeds they will produce plants that have all the characteristics of gloxinias, generation after generation. All gloxinias, no matter what their color, belong to the same species, *Sinningia speciosa.*

Sinningia speciosa

Although the species is the smallest *natural* group to which a plant belongs, smaller subdivisions within the species are often recognized. For cultivated plants, these subgroups are nearly always maintained by vegetative propagation and are called *cultivars* (varieties). Cultivar names are generally not in Latin and are not written in italics or underlined. They are, however, capitalized. They are written after the species name using the abbreviation *cv.* or simply single quotation marks, as in these examples:

Sinningia speciosa cv. Hollywood
Sinningia speciosa 'Hollywood'
Sinningia speciosa cv. Princess Elizabeth
Sinningia speciosa 'Princess Elizabeth'

Sinningia speciosa plants (gloxinias) having flowers of different colors can thus be distinguished from one another by giving each kind a cultivar name. But they still belong to the same species, and if they were cross-pollinated and the resulting seeds planted, the offspring would have flowers of many different colors. In order to maintain cultivars, therefore, they must be propagated vegetatively to prevent genetic recombination of characteristics within the species.

A few plants in this book are *subspecies* and not varieties. Examples are *Codiaeum variegatum pictum* and *Asparagus asparagoides myrtifolius.*

Review. To see if you understand plant classification, insert the names of the missing taxonomical groups for a common indoor plant, jade plant, *Crassula argentea.*

Subkingdom *Embryophyta*
 Phylum
  Subphylum
   Class
    Subclass
     Order   Rosales
      Family   Crassulaceae
       Genus
        Species

PLANT ECOLOGY AND PLANT PHYSIOLOGY

Since horticulture covers many different kinds of plants requiring different cultural techniques, our emphasis will be basic plant ecology and physiology. Plant ecology is the study of the relations of plants to their environment. Plant physiology is concerned with the functions of living plants.

The various external conditions or factors which influence the growth structure and reproduction of plants are collectively spoken of as the environment. The natural environment of a plant is always changing; the intensity of environmental factors varies with the hour, the day, and the season. These factors can be subdivided into:

Light
Temperature
Water
Atmospheric gases
Growing media

Before studying how these individual factors influence plants, however, a review of plant physiology must be made.

Plant Physiology

Movement of Water and Nutrients into Plants. Water moves into a plant mainly through root hairs, which are outgrowths from the epidermal cells near the root tip. The supply of water and mineral nutrients at the surface of root hairs growing through the soil involves the process of *diffusion.* This is the spreading out of the molecules of a gas, liquid, or solid through all of the space that they can reach from a place of high concentration to places of lower concentration. If a lump of sugar were dropped into a cup of water, the sugar would slowly dissolve. The molecules of sugar would slowly move to the areas of lower concentration. The water in the cup does not have to be stirred for the movement of the molecules to take place. After a time, the lump of sugar disappears and the sugar molecules become evenly distributed throughout the cup. To speed this action up, you commonly use a spoon to stir the coffee after adding sugar.

Water and mineral nutrients enter the cell by the process of osmosis. *Osmosis* is the diffusion of water through a differentially permeable membrane from a region of higher water concentration to a region of lower water concentration. A *differentially permeable membrane* is one which allows certain substances to pass through, and which prohibits or restricts the passage of other substances. Nutrient elements dissolved in water can move into the plant with the water. It is principally through the process of osmosis that water moves into the living cells of a plant and from one living cell to another.

Water and dissolved materials move up the root into the stem and on up into the leaves. The plant tissue through which the water and dissolved materials are transported is called *xylem*. The annual rings in a tree are xylem tissue.

The upward movement of water and dissolved substances in plants is best explained by the *cohesion theory*, which can be summarized as follows. The evaporation of water (*transpiration*) from leaves causes a water deficit in the leaf cells. This deficit results in a pull which is transmitted downward to adjacent cells into the roots. The cohesive power of water molecules is strong enough to withstand this pull. Water and nutrients are thus said to move in the "transpiration stream."

Photosynthesis. The principle function of leaves is *photosynthesis*—the manufacture of sugar from carbon dioxide from the air and water from the soil in the presence of chlorophyll and light energy. Oxygen is released during the process.

$$6CO_2 + 12H_2O + \frac{light}{chlorophyll} \rightarrow C_6H_{12}O_6 + 6O_2 + 6H_2O$$

$$\text{Carbon dioxide} + \text{water} + \frac{light}{chlorophyll} \rightarrow \text{sugar} + \text{oxygen} + \text{water}$$

Starch is usually the first visible product of photosynthesis. The presence of starch can easily be tested for by boiling leaves in alcohol to extract the chlorophyll and then applying iodine to the leaf. If the leaves have been carrying on photosynthesis at a rapid rate, much of the sugar manufactured should have been converted and stored as starch. If starch is present, the leaves should turn dark blue or brown when treated with iodine.

Transpiration. The greater part of the water (perhaps 95%) absorbed by the roots of plants passes through the plant unchanged and is lost from the above-ground parts of the plant (chiefly leaves) in the form of water vapor. Water loss from leaves is primarily through stomata. A much smaller amount of water is lost through the cuticle which covers the leaf epidermis. Only small quantities of water are actually used in growth and as a raw material in photosynthesis.

Respiration. The process by which the stored energy of a soluble food is released for use by a plant is called *respiration* and occurs at *all* times in *all* living cells. A generalized equation for aerobic respiration is:

$$C_6H_{12}O_6 + 6O_2 \longrightarrow 6H_2O + 6CO_2 + 674 \text{ calories}$$
$$\text{Sugar} + \text{oxygen} \longrightarrow \text{water} + \text{carbon dioxide} + \text{energy}$$

Digestion. The process by which insoluble foods stored in plants are made soluble is called *digestion.* All foods contain stored energy, but before this energy can be made available for growth, the food must be in a soluble state. Foods stored in an insoluble form, such as starch or protein, can neither be used in the cells in which they are stored nor translocated to other parts of the plant until they have been changed to a soluble and diffusible form by enzymatic action. *Translocation* is the movement of foods or mineral solutes from one part of a plant to another. Complex insoluble foods which are broken down by either respiration or digestion into simpler foods may then be combined in various ways to form other types of compounds such as oils, fats, and cellulose.

Plant Growth Regulators. Several plant hormones, natural or synthetic, are being used in the production and propagation of horticultural plants and products. Some of these hormones can be purchased in garden stores and used by the homeowner. Plant growth regulators are "chemical messengers" which affect plant growth and development. The term "plant growth regulator" includes both the natural chemical messengers (hormones) and the commercially available synthetic materials. Several chemicals induce root formation on cuttings; others sprayed on plants reduce their height; while others, on the contrary, can increase plant growth.

The hormones can be divided into several groups according to the similarity of their effects: auxins, gibberellins, cytokinins, growth retardants, and a miscellaneous group which includes ethylene and others.

Auxins were discovered in the 1930's after it had been noted that the coleoptile (a protective sheath around the first leaves of grasses) of *Avena* (oat) contained a substance which caused the cells of the coleoptile to elongate. If the tip of the coleoptile was removed, no elongation occurred. If the tip was cut off and placed on one side of the coleoptile, a negative curving occurred (that is, a curvature away from the side of the applied tip). The agent which caused cell elongation was extracted from several sources and was found to be universal in the plant kingdom. It turned out to be indoleacetic acid, commonly known as IAA, which is responsible for this response in plants.

Soon a whole group of derivatives was discovered to have a similar formula. They are used as rooting hormones on cuttings, as herbicides, and more recently as defoliants in combat zones. Other rooting hormones are IBA (indolebutyric acid) and NAA (napthaleneacetic acid). Commonly, IBA is used for the rooting of cuttings because it has a stronger effect than IAA. IBA can be obtained in garden supply stores under such names as Rootone and Hormodin. Hormones are commonly used to promote rooting on only a few houseplants such as grape ivy, kangaroo vine, rubber plant, fiddle-leaf fig, and other woody or slow-rooting plants.

Some herbicides such as 2,4-D and 2,4,5-T exhibit auxin-like activity. They cause a plant to grow very vigorously with twisted malformed leaves. Monocots (grasses, corn, wheat, etc.) are less susceptible to herbicides, and this provides a method to eliminate broadleaved weeds (dicots) from lawns, corn fields, wheat fields, and other places.

Of all the plant hormones, auxins have found the largest practical application. Some other areas in which auxins are used are the prevention of the sprouting of potato tubers (during their storage) and the prevention of fruit formation on ornamental trees (horse chestnut, honey locust, and female ginkgo trees).

Gibberellins are natural plant hormones. They were discovered in Japan at the same time as the auxins, but their discovery reached the western world in the 1950's, both because the research was published in Japanese and because there were poor communications during World War II. Gibberellic acid (commonly abbreviated as GA) was discovered in rice (produced by a fungus). It caused rice plants to grow excessively, resulting in the so-called Foolish Disease of rice. Various derivatives and compounds with gibberellic-acid-like activity are now known. There are more than thirty gibberellins, all with very similar formulas.

Hopes for finding many practical uses were once high because, when applied to plants, gibberellins caused the internodes to elongate tremendously, and leaf and flower size increased many times. Ideas about "wonder crops" arose, but unfortunately, gibberellins did not find as many practical applications as the auxins. Now GA's are used to spray grapes to increase the berry size, to restore the damage caused by a late frost—through formation of parthenocarpic fruits (produced without fertilization) of the pear (Europe)—and in the brewing industry. In floriculture, GA is used to a lesser extent. It can be put to use in growing standard trees of geraniums, lantanas, and fuchsias. The apex of the plant is sprayed weekly, or GA on a cotton ball is applied to the apex. All side shoots are removed and when the desired height is reached, the application is stopped. The terminal bud is removed to induce branching, and the lower leaves are stripped off when the top of the plant has formed enough branches. Another method of applying gibberellins is to spray the buds of geraniums with a very low concentration—1 to 10 parts per million (ppm)—to prolong the life of the inflorescence.

Kinetin, which was discovered recently, has no practical application so far; it was once thought to be the agent which caused cell division to occur. A synthetic kinetin is BA (benzyladenine), but it also has no practical application to date. Kinetin retards the senescence (aging) of chlorophyll in leaves that have been cut off the plant. It has been tested as a post-harvest treatment of vegetables.

Growth retardants have found a wide-spread use in floriculture because they can shorten the stems of pot plants like poinsettias, chrysanthemums, gardenias, and azaleas. Growth retardants are synthetically manufactured chemicals and are often not intentionally discovered. Their formulas do not have much similarity with each other. Some commonly used retardants include Phosphon, B-9 (also known as Alar or SADH), CCC or Cycocel, and MH (maleic hydrazide). The chemicals are sprayed on the plants in one to three applications. (Phosphon is an exception because it is applied to the soil, where it is very persistent. When the treated soil is used again for potting of other plants, dwarfing will occur.) MH is sometimes applied to lawns or sprayed on trees or hedges to retard the growth.

Ethylene was recently added to the list of plant hormones. A commercial preparation which releases ethylene is Ethephon (ethrel). One of the mechanisms of auxin application is the production of ethylene, and this method is used to induce flowering in the bromeliads, the family to which the pineapple belongs. If NAA is applied in the "vase" of the pineapple, flowering will occur. At home, this technique can be copied to force mature bromeliads (aechmea, vriesia, pineapples, etc.) to flower. Since ethylene is also produced by ripening apples, an apple can be used. Place the bromeliad and the apple in a tightly closed plastic bag for a few days.

Tropisms. A *tropism* is a bending of a part of a plant which is caused by differences in growth rate as induced by external stimuli. For example, in *phototropism*, light is the external stimulus. In *geotropism*, gravity is the external stimulus.

Stems bend towards light because the cells in the stem are growing at different rates. The growth-regulating substances called auxins are produced in buds, stem tips, young leaves, and embryos. Auxins produced at the tips of stems move down the stem and are broken down by light on the lighted side and, in addition, accumulate in the darkened side of the stem faster than in the side exposed to light. Some auxin may also be distributed from the light side to the dark side. This higher concentration of auxin results in the increased growth of cells on the dark side. The phototropic reaction would be a *positive* reaction in that the stem bends toward light.

Geotropism is a growth movement induced by a gravitational stimulus. Roots show a *positive* geotropic reaction. The mechanism here is similar to that in the stem. In roots, however, the increased concentration of auxin retards growth. Therefore, if you place a root horizontally on the ground, the auxin will diffuse to the lower part of the root because of gravity. The increased concentration of auxin then retards growth on the lower side. The upper side of the root does grow, however, and since the lower side does not, or grows at a slower rate, the root will bend downward.

Environmental Factors Affecting Plant Growth

1. Light

Light influences the growth of plants through its effects on photosynthesis, transpiration, flowering, soil temperature, enzyme action, rate of water absorption, etc. Its *quality* (wavelength or color), *intensity* (measured in footcandles), and *duration* (day length or *photoperiod)* are all important.

Quality. When light is passed through a prism, it is separated into wavelengths of different colors (the colors of the rainbow):

400 - 435 millimicrons*	violet
435 - 490	blue
490 - 574	green
574 - 595	yellow
595 - 626	orange
626 - 750	red

The light reactions of the plant (photosynthesis,

---

*A micron is 1/1000 of a millimeter; a millimicron is 1/1000 of a micron or 1/1,000,000 of a millimeter.

phototropism, photoperiodism) are based on photo-
chemical reactions carried on by specific pigment
systems that respond to various wavelengths. For
example, violet, blue, and green are important in
phototropism responses. Red and blue are important
in the photosynthetic process. Orange and red are
important in the photoperiodic reaction.

Intensity. Light quantity or intensity refers to the
concentration of light waves. The maximum light
intensity at noon on a clear day out-of-doors is about
10,000 footcandles. Light intensity affects most of
the processes that are carried on by plants. In photosynthesis, with an increase in light intensity there is
generally an increase in the rate of photosynthesis
until some other factor becomes limiting. Maximum
rates of photosynthesis are obtained in the leaves of
most plants at light intensities considerably below
that of full sunlight, probably in the neighborhood of
one-third to one-fourth full sunlight. Very low light
intensities, however, are effective in inducing a phototropic response.

The effect of light intensity on vegetative growth
can be summarized as follows. Relatively high light
intensity results in shorter internodes, shorter plants,
and smaller leaves, but the dry weight of the plant is
greater than under lower light intensities. The size of
the root system and the number of flowers and fruits
are also greater under the higher intensities. Seedlings
which develop in the absence of light have whitish
or yellowish spindly stems and relatively poorly
developed root systems and are commonly described
as being *etiolated*.

Duration (Photoperiodism). Flowering in plants
may be caused by a number of conditions. One
condition that is important for several florist's crops
and houseplants is light duration or day length.
Plants that flower in response to day length are said
to exhibit *photoperiodism*. Some plants flower when
the days are long, and others when the days are short.
They are called *long-day plants* and *short-day plants*
respectively. Actually, they should be called short-
night and long-night plants since it really is the period
of uninterrupted darkness that is important.

Chrysanthemums, poinsettias, gardenias, and the
Christmas cactus are all short-day (or long-night)
plants. They will flower after they have been exposed
to a certain number of short days. Such plants
normally flower in late fall or winter, when the days

are naturally short. They can be induced to flower in other seasons by pulling a special light-proof black cloth or plastic around them in order to artificially shorten the day length. It is very important that such plants have a long uninterrupted night in order for them to flower properly. Even a few minutes of artificial light during this period is enough to disrupt flowering. People who seem to have a lot of "luck" in blooming the Christmas cactus usually keep it in a spare room or other place where plants do not get any light at night.

The formation of bulbs and tubers is also controlled by day length. Tuberous-rooted begonia, which is a long-day plant for flowering, produces tubers on short days but not on long days. Onions, on the other hand, produce bulbs on long days, but not when the days are short. *Dormancy*—a state of rest or inactivity—is another plant response regulated by photoperiod.

2. Temperature

Growing plants are constantly influenced by variations in the temperature, both of the soil in which they grow and of the surrounding air. Most plants grow best in a temperature range of 70° to 90°F and cease growth when air and soil temperatures approach freezing or rise much above 100°F. Structures such as seeds, however, are much more resistant to extremes of temperature than are active organs because seeds have a lower water content.

Plants often are divided into two groups based on their temperature requirements. *Warm season* plants (tropical or subtropical in origin) thrive at temperatures above 70°F, stop growth around 50°F, and are very sensitive to frost or cold temperatures. *Cool season* plants (temperate in origin) thrive at temperatures below 70°F, are frost tolerant, and stop growth or are killed by high temperatures. These groupings also apply to optimum germination temperatures.

Plants which are able to survive exposure to subfreezing temperatures are termed *hardy*. Examples of hardy plants are asparagus, peonies, apples, and tulips. Hardiness varies as to species and is subject to considerable modification by variance in environmental conditions. Plants grown in greenhouses or protected areas should be "hardened off" before being placed outside or in the home, so that they will be conditioned to withstand the changes in temperature, humidity, light, and air movement.

Temperature also affects the dormancy of flower buds. Apples, peaches, biennials, and spring-flowering bulbs grown in warmer climates without low winter temperatures usually do not flower unless they are exposed to temperatures over 80°F.

3. Water

In order for physiological functions to take place inside a plant, plant cells are continually taking in certain materials and allowing others to pass out. The ability of cells to act in this manner is necessary before any other processes can take place.

Of all the substances which enter plant cells, water is fundamentally important. It is an essential constituent of protoplasm and is a raw material in photosynthesis. It is the liquid in which solid materials must ordinarily be dissolved before they can enter or leave a cell or move from one portion of a plant to another. Water is the medium in which most of the chemical reactions of protoplasm occur. It also provides the internal pressure for the maintenance and form of the growth of cells. Usually 80% to 90% of the fresh weight of a plant or plant part is water. The remaining 10% to 20% is the solid material of the plant and is mostly carbohydrate.

Most species of plants possess minimum, maximum, and optimum soil moisture concentrations which influence their growth. Plants may be stunted in their development by too much water as well as by too little water. Plant water stress occurs whenever the water loss from plants (transpiration) is greater than uptake (absorption).

Several terms are used in describing the amount of water in soil. *Field capacity* is the amount of water in soil after a thorough rain. The amount of water remaining in soil at the point when a plant wilts and can't recover is called the *permanent wilting point*. The amount of water in soil between the field capacity and the permanent wilting point is called *available moisture*. Further information on watering is included in the section About Watering.

4. Atmospheric Gases

Oxygen is required for normal root growth and for respiration. Carbon dioxide is a raw material of photosynthesis, and therefore its presence is necessary in the manufacture of carbohydrates. A moderate increase in the carbon dioxide content of air usually accelerates photosynthetic activity.

Plants are dependent upon soil for anchorage, water, and nutrients. The root system of a plant may even be larger than the top of the plant.

The two basic types of soil are *mineral* and *organic*. Mineral soils are composed of inorganic substances and varying amounts of decaying organic matter. Organic soils (such as muck and peat) are formed from partly decayed plant materials. Soil *texture* refers to the proportion of gravel, sand, silt, and clay particles in the soil. Soils containing significant amounts of each are termed *loam*. Soil *structure* refers to the arrangement of the soil particles.

The soil is also the source of mineral elements. The inorganic materials of the soil which are insoluble in water are brought in solution by acids produced during the decay of organic materials and by other agencies. The essential elements in non-living organic matter are released by the activities of the microscopic organisms of the soil, chiefly bacteria and fungi. The essential elements are not found in elementary form in the soil water, nor do they occur in elementary form when they are added as fertilizer. They occur in the soil as *ions* (atoms or groups of atoms carrying positive or negative electrical charges). Plants may exhibit deficiencies of some of the essential elements even though such elements are abundant in the soil. An excess of certain elements may prevent the absorption of others, or the elements may be present in an insoluble form. The degree of acidity or alkalinity (pH) of the growing medium is frequently the chief factor which determines whether an element is insoluble or not.

Essential elements are those chemical elements present in the soil and air which are necessary for normal plant growth and development, as either a component of the plant's structure or a requirement for physiological processes to function. At the present time, there are at least 16 elements which are considered essential for the growth of higher plants. Those elements needed in relatively large amounts by plants are termed *macroelements* and include nitrogen (N), potassium (K), calcium (Ca), phosphorus (P), magnesium (Mg), sulfur (S), iron (Fe), carbon (C), hydrogen (H), and oxygen (O). Elements needed only in minute quantities are termed *microelements* and include chlorine (Cl), copper (Cu), manganese (Mn), zinc (Zn), molybdenum (Mo), and boron (B). Carbon, hydrogen, and oxygen are from the air and water. The other elements are obtained from the soil.

Nitrogen is a constituent of all proteins and is also present in the chlorophyll molecule. Phosphorus is present in nucleoproteins and plays an important role in many enzymatic reactions. Potassium seems to be essential in the formation and translocation of carbohydrates. Calcium plays a major role in cell wall formations.

Sulfur is a component of some proteins and amino acids that are essential to normal plant metabolism. Magnesium is a component of the chlorophyll molecule and is therefore essential for the chlorophyll formation. Boron probably plays a part in cell wall formation and in the translocation of sugars. Iron is necessary for the formation of chlorophyll, though it is not a part of the chlorophyll molecule.

Manganese is also essential for chlorophyll formation without being a part of the chlorophyll molecule. Zinc is present in enzymes and is necessary for chlorophyll formation; it also plays a part in the synthesis of hormones. Molybdenum is a component of an enzyme involved in nitrate reduction in the plant. Copper is a component of certain enzymes that function in oxidation reactions.

Soil alone is a relatively poor growing medium due to poor drainage and aeration, and shrinking and cracking when dry. For these and other reasons, soils for growing horticultural plants are usually amended with such materials as peat moss, vermiculite, perlite and sand. Media composed only of these components are termed *artificial* or *synthetic* growing mixes or media. Several synthetic media are available commercially, for example, Jiffy Mix, Pro Mix, and Peat Lite, which contain peat moss, vermiculite, and/or perlite.

One of the most common soil-amended media is a 1:1:1 mixture by volume of loam, peat moss, and sand or perlite. One of the main advantages of using a soil-amended medium instead of an artificial medium is that soil-amended media have a greater nutrient-holding capacity and, therefore, have a greater reserve of nutrients for the plant to draw upon.

Plant care

GENERAL PLANT CARE

Fertilizing Plants Grown Indoors

Many soil mixes used for indoor plant culture incorporate large amounts of inorganic materials such as vermiculite and perlite, which have very little nutrient value. Such mixes are often referred to as *amended* mixes. Media which contain no soil (artificial or synthetic media) are very, very low in nutrient value. Fertilization of these media is extremely important. One of the most popular artificial media is the peat-lite mix, which contains an equal volume of peat moss and vermiculite or perlite. Peat-lite mixes normally include limestone, superphosphate, borax, chelated iron, and a complete fertilizer such as 5-10-5 or 5-10-10.

A *complete fertilizer* is one that contains all three major elements—nitrogen, phosphorus, and potassium. These are the nutrients most often needed by plants in large quantities. The numbers on a bag or box of fertilizer indicate how much nitrogen, phosphorus, and potassium are in the fertilizer. If a bag is marked 5-10-5, it means that 5% of the mixture inside the container by weight is nitrogen (N), 10% is phosphorus (usually listed as available P_2O_5), and 5% is potassium (usually listed as K_2O). The rest of the mixture is made up of other elements and filler materials which help keep the mixture from getting hard and from separating. The order of the nutrients in the numbers on the container is alphabetical—nitrogen, phosphorus, potassium.

Although several different nutrients are usually added to the soil mixes when they are prepared, most indoor plants will benefit by periodic applications of a complete fertilizer such as 20-20-20 or any other common houseplant fertilizer.

31

Fertilizers come in several different forms such as granular or powder, liquid, slow-release pellets, and tablets or pills. Probably the form used by most houseplant growers is the granular or powder form that is instantly soluble in water. Another form is liquid, which comes ready to use. A third form, used especially by commercial growers, is slow-release pellets like Osmocote. The advantage of this form is that fertilizer is being released slowly over a long period of time (several months) from just one application so that the plants don't need to be fertilized as often.

Fertilization of indoor plants should be done according to the directions on the container. Probably the most common recommendation for fertilizing indoor plants is to fertilize them once a month at a concentration recommended by the manufacturer, or twice a month at half the concentration for monthly fertilization. Do not fertilize plants when they are dormant. Cacti, for example, usually grow very slowly in the winter months and should not be fertilized during this period.

Fertilizing plants is commonly done by applying a fertilizer solution instead of water. It is usually recommended that the soil be moist before fertilizing. Add enough of the solution to thoroughly wet the entire soil mass just as you would during a regular watering. Any excess solution that drains out the bottom of the pot can be discarded. If the fertilizer solution gets on the foliage, be sure to wash the foliage off.

It should also be noted that plants which have attained sufficient size to be useful in a home, room, or other setting may not need to be fertilized periodically. This is especially true for larger plants that have attained the maximum size for a particular location. In situations such as this where extra growth is not desired, fertilizing should be kept to a minimum and done only enough to keep the foliage from turning light green or yellow. Plants growing slowly, as under low light conditions, will also not need fertilizing as frequently as plants that are growing vigorously.

The method of fertilizer application to use depends on personal preference, convenience, equipment, cost, and availability. An easy way to compare costs is to add up the numbers on the label, multiply this figure (percentage) by the quantity in the container which gives you the actual amount of nutrients (N,P,K) in the container by weight. Then divide the cost by the weight of the nutrients, and the result is the cost per unit for each fertilizer.

A very common and serious mistake is to overfertilize plants. Overfertilization results in excess soluble salt concentration in the media. Plant stems may be burned near the surface of the growing medium, and often a white crust can be seen on the medium surface or on the outside of the clay pots. Excess soluble salts withhold water from plants; therefore, wilting is often a symptom of this problem.

The level of soluble salts in a growing medium is determined by an electrical conductivity test of a water suspension of the medium. Excess soluble salts in a growing medium can be partially removed by occasionally flooding the medium with water, a process called *leaching*. Leaching is especially important for plants that are watered from below since there is a great chance for the buildup of soluble salts. Some soluble salts are flushed out the bottom of the pot when it is watered from above.

Examples of the four different forms of fertilizer and their costs are given on page 34.

These figures are, of course, only rough comparisons and may not represent relationships between different forms of fertilizers. In general, fertilizers containing a higher percentage of nitrogen will probably cost more since nitrogen is usually more expensive than phosphorus and potassium. It should also be pointed out that some of these fertilizers include more minor elements than others.

A more precise method of determining costs or making comparisons would be by comparing only the elements. The atomic weights of phosphorus, oxygen, and potassium are 31, 16, and 39 respectively, so P_2O_5 is actually 43.6% phosphorus $\left(\dfrac{62}{62+80}\right)$, and K_2O is 83% potassium $\left(\dfrac{78}{78+16}\right)$ Nitrogen remains unchanged. One thing that should be noted from this table is that the cost per pound decreases substantially as the quantity increases.

The following statements summarize this section on fertilizing plants:

1. Most plants will benefit by being fertilized periodically, especially those being grown in artificial soil mixes.
2. Do not fertilize dormant plants.
3. There are many different forms of fertilizer available for fertilizing plants.
4. Fertilize according to instructions on the label (do not overfertilize).

Pinching Plants

The tip of a growing shoot produces the hormone auxin which travels down the stem and inhibits the development of lateral buds. This inhibiting effect of the apical (tip) bud over lateral buds is called *apical dominance*. When the tip of the shoot is pinched off, the axillary buds are no longer inhibited

COMPARISON OF FERTILIZER COSTS

Type or Form of Fertilizer	Analysis	Weight	Cost ($)	Total Combined Analysis (%)	Total Weight of N, P, K (lbs.)	Cost per Pound ($ ÷ wt.)
Tablets	20-10-5	25 x 21 g. (453.6 g./lb.)	3.25	35 (20 + 10 + 5)	.405 $\left(\frac{35 \times 25 \times 21}{453.6} = .405\right)$	8.02 $\left(\frac{3.25}{.405}\right)$
Slow release	14-14-14	3 lbs.	4.65	42	.42 x 3 = 1.26	3.69
	14-14-14	12 lbs.	16.95	42	.42 x 12 = 5.04	3.36
Water-soluble granular	12-31-14	8 oz.	1.55	57	.57 x .5 = .285	5.44
	12-31-14	1 lb.	2.95	57	.57 x 1 = .57	5.18
	12-31-14	2.5 lbs.	5.30	57	.57 x 2.5 = 1.425	3.72
	12-31-14	5 lbs.	7.95	57	.57 x 5 = 2.85	2.79
	20-20-20	8 oz.	1.67	60	.60 x .5 = .3	5.50
	20-20-20	2 lbs.	4.15	60	.60 x 2 = 1.2	3.46
	23-19-17	2 lbs.	3.49	59	.59 x 2 = 1.18	2.95
	23-19-17	5 lbs.	6.95	59	.59 x 5 = 2.95	2.35
Liquid	12-6-6	1 qt.	2.69	24	.24 x 2 = .48	5.60

and they can develop into lateral shoots. The result is a more bushy, compact plant. Pinching fast-growing upright plants such as coleus or iresine will keep them down to a more manageable size and improve their appearance. Only plants having conspicuous stems can be pinched; plants like the African violet, snake plant, and pick-a-back cannot. Although most vines can be pinched once to make them more compact, it is usually better to place three or more plants in the same pot so that they will fill in the base more quickly.

Begin pinching before a plant starts to look leggy. Use your thumb and forefinger to remove the terminal bud. If you wait too long, you will have to include part of the internode and perhaps one or more nodes. You should try to pinch early so that you remove only a very small portion of the growing tip. You will have to pinch growing tips repeatedly to keep most plants bushy. Fingernail clippers can sometimes be used to pinch out small terminal buds before they are large enough to be pinched by hand. Continue pinching lateral branches to maintain a compact plant. If you let a plant go too long before pinching, pinch low enough (and rather severely) to avoid a top-heavy effect. Pinch just *above* a bud in order to not leave unsightly stumps, but be careful not to damage the bud. The portion of the stem removed can be used as a cutting if it is large enough.

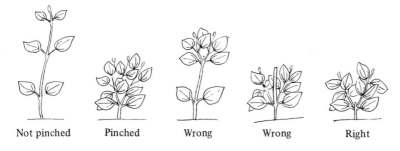

Not pinched   Pinched   Wrong   Wrong   Right

Axillary buds may develop into leafy shoots or flowering shoots. In some flowering plants, all flower buds on the stem except the terminal one may be removed. This process is called *disbudding*. As a result the single shoot becomes very tall, and the flower that develops from the single bud is much larger than it would be if other flower buds were allowed to develop. Disbudding is a common horticultural practice in the culture of roses, carnations, and football chrysanthemums.

Grooming Plants

Houseplants need continuous care and maintenance to insure their lasting appeal and beauty. In addition to routine practices of watering, fertilizing, repotting, pinching, and controlling pests, there are several other things to be done to keep plants looking healthy: removing dead or dying leaves and flowers, cleaning leaves, rotating plants so they don't bend toward light and become misshapen, pulling up weeds, and so forth.

It is normal for the lower leaves of many plants to die and fall off as the plant grows and puts out new leaves. Hopefully, this leaf drop will occur slowly if the plant is properly cared for. Remove lower leaves as they turn brown or yellow.

Many plants have leaf tips that have become brown and brittle. These brown leaf tips can be removed by breaking or cutting them off with a pair of shears. If you want, you can cut the tips off at an angle to make them resemble healthy leaves instead of just cutting them off straight across the blade.

Special Cultural Requirements

Most common houseplants will grow indoors under average household conditions. It is much easier for most indoor gardeners to learn and remember the exceptions to this broad statement than to attempt to memorize the specific cultural requirements for each and every plant, unless only a few species are to be grown.

Some of the special cultural requirements that indoor plant growers need to be aware of in order to grow plants successfully are humidity, light, and porosity of the growing medium. In general, most plants will grow best under high light intensities, high humidity, and in a rather porous growing medium. Many plants will exist or survive under low light conditions and low humidity, but won't grow as well.

Humidity. Most houseplants will grow best at a much higher humidity than can be attained or maintained in most homes heated by hot air in winter (December through February) in northern climates. Condensation on windowpanes and aluminum frames occurs at about 35% relative humidity when the outdoor temperature is below freezing. Therefore, even if a good power humidifier is used, the relative humidity can seldom be greater than 40% because moisture in the air will condense on cold surfaces such as windowpanes. About the only disadvantages of high humidity are: the soil that plants are growing in won't dry out as fast, because of lower transpiration rates; and disease organisms may become more of a problem.

Light. Houseplants are often divided into two groups based mainly on their light requirements. Flowering plants usually require higher light intensities than do foliage plants.

Plants grown under low light tend to be tall and leggy (etiolated) and flowering types may fail to bloom. Leaves of plants receiving too much light will be burned.

Light intensity is often a limiting factor when plants are grown indoors. Although the intensity is usually high enough on windowsills or near windows if the windows are not shaded by trees or buildings, the intensity drops drastically as you move away from windows. The intensity also varies depending upon the exposure, with southern exposures receiving the most light and northern exposures receiving the least. The intensity also varies from summer to winter. Therefore, when selecting plants for areas which receive low light, it will normally be best to select foliage-type plants unless supplemental light is added.

The light intensity that plants receive indoors is usually broken down into categories.

Category	Examples	Light Intensity
High or full sun	South window	1,000 to 10,000 foot-candles
Medium light or partial sun	East or west window	200 to 4,000 foot-candles
Low light or shady	North window or interior of room	50 to 500 footcandles

These categories are not very precise, however, because they vary by season (summer vs. winter) and whether a particular day is sunny or overcast.

Artificial Lighting. Since the light intensity indoors is much lower than out-of-doors, it is often necessary to provide supplemental light when growing plants indoors. The two basic types of artificial lighting available are *incandescent* and *fluorescent*.

Incandescent lights have several distinct disadvantages when used alone. First, they emit only about one-third to one-fifth the amount of light of a comparably sized fluorescent bulb. For example, a 40-watt incandescent tube gives off about 465 lumens and a 40-watt fluorescent tube gives off about 2,500 lumens. Second, it will cost more to burn incandescent bulbs because about three to five times as many watts will be needed. Third, the heat radiated can be a problem because it can burn or scorch plants. Fourth, incandescent bulbs do not burn as long as fluorescent bulbs (perhaps only one-tenth as long). Lastly, the light quality of the common incandescent bulb provides an excess of red light and is low in blue light.

Fluorescent bulbs are most commonly used for supplementing light indoors because they emit more light per watt, are cheaper to operate, produce less heat (usually an advantage), burn longer (tubes should be replaced before they burn out because their efficiency decreases), and come in a wide range of bulb types. The common cool white bulb provides an excess of blue light.

Special fluorescent bulbs for plants are available that provide sufficient red and blue light for photosynthesis, including Gro-Lux, Plant-Gro, and Plant Light. Some disadvantages of these special lights are that they are often hard to find, and they are often considerably more expensive than the standard cool white bulbs. They often are not described in detail, nor are definite specifications included with them so that the purchaser knows the quality and amount of light that the tube will give off.

Most indoor gardeners will probably find that the standard cool white fluorescent bulb will be satisfactory for growing most indoor plants if their plants receive some natural light through windows. If cool white bulbs do not prove satisfactory by themselves, replacing half of them with daylight fluorescent bulbs should be beneficial. Or, using the cool white fluorescent bulbs in combination with incandescent bulbs in the ratio of about 1 watt of incandescent light to 3 watts of fluorescent light should prove satisfactory. Some fluorescent light fixtures have sockets for incandescent bulbs. (Probably the most common fixture is one that will hold two 40-watt fluorescent bulbs and two incandescent bulbs, the 25-watt size being recommended.)

If you need to buy fluorescent fixtures, the size that holds 40-watt bulbs 4 feet long, or the 8-foot length, are usually the most economical to buy when you consider the amount of space or number of plants that they can light. Some of these fixtures will hold four fluorescent bulbs instead of just two, which would be desirable if you planned to use the fixture primarily for starting seeds. Seedlings tend to get very leggy when the light intensity is low.

Supplemental light should be provided for 12 to 16 hours a day when natural light is low or nonexistent. In winter months, most plants other than those with a southern exposure will benefit from the addition of supplemental light in late afternoon or evening so that they will receive a total of 12 to 16 hours of light daily.

A standard fluorescent fixture that has only two 40-watt tubes will provide about 850 footcandles when placed 6 inches above plants, 500 footcandles at 1 foot above plants, 250 footcandles at 2 feet, and 100 footcandles at 3 feet. With a standard reflector, the area lighted will be about 2 feet wide and 4 feet long.

Growing Medium. The porosity of the growing medium is especially important because the most common way of killing houseplants is by overwatering. It is much easier to kill plants grown in a medium that retains a lot of moisture than it is in one that retains only a moderate amount.

Hardening Off. Most houseplants are grown in green-houses or nurseries where watering, temperature, light, and humidity are usually at optimum levels. Taking a plant that was produced under almost ideal conditions and placing it in the atmosphere of most homes, apartments, dormitories, or offices is a great shock. Some plants never survive this move. Others respond by dropping lower leaves and/or flowers (or buds); some die back from the top.

There are several things that indoor gardeners can do to reduce the shock of moving tender plants from an almost ideal environment to an environment that is rather harsh. The process called *hardening off* normally refers to getting plants ready for outdoors (particularly bedding plants), but the principles of hardening off also apply to the transfer of houseplants from one environment to another. The process is also referred to as *acclimatization*.

Most commercial plant growers start the hardening off process by gradually exposing plants to more air circulation, lower humidity, and perhaps less frequent watering. With the strong demand for plants, this process may have been shortened considerably. Regardless, most flowering and foliage plants should be given special treatment for the first few weeks after purchase. To help plants adjust to low humidity, mist them occasionally, group them together on moistened gravel, cover them with plastic, and, in general, just try to raise the normal level of the humidity indoors·for a few days to a couple of weeks.

To help new plants adjust to different levels of light intensity, gradually expose them to the levels at which you plan to grow them. If their new home is in a south-facing window, start exposing them to full sunlight for only a half hour or so, early or late in the day. After a few days, start increasing the length of exposure until they are receiving full sunlight for the entire day, but be on the lookout for leaf burn from too much sun.

Summer Care of Potted Plants. Many indoor plant growers move their potted plants outdoors in the summer. It is usually easier to care for them if they are grouped together in the shade where they receive some protection from breezes. A garden hose can be used for the watering, which will probably have to be done more frequently than indoors.

Porous pots can be sunken into the ground to reduce moisture loss through the sides. Plants should be brought back indoors before frost in the fall.

GROWTH PREFERENCES FOR INDOOR PLANTS

	Special Conditions for a Few Plants	*Most Plants Grow Best under These Conditions*	*Special Conditions for a Few Plants*
TEMPERATURE	Cool (below 60°F) ---------------------------- Cyclamen, azalea, begonias, English ivy, fatshedera, Norfolk Island pine, pittosporum, podocarpus	60° to 75°F during the day and 10° to 15° cooler at night	Hot (above 75°F) ---------------------------- Many cacti, succulents, and other indoor plants will tolerate high temperatures.
HUMIDITY	Dry to slightly moist (5% to 40% relative humidity). Humidity in most homes heated by hot air in winter in northern climates usually falls within this range. ---------------------------- Most cacti and succulents will normally survive in a very dry atmosphere.	40% to 80% relative humidity. Moderately humid to very humid. This level of humidity usually cannot be attained indoors in winter in northern areas heated by hot air.	Very humid (above 80% relative humidity) ---------------------------- Fittonia and other terrarium plants will normally survive this very humid condition.
LIGHT INTENSITY	Low light (deep shade) ---------------------------- Chinese evergreen, some ferns, ficus, cast-iron plant	Light shade to bright light (intensities vary as to season of year and are highest during the summer). Intensities are highest for southern exposures and lowest for northern exposures.	High light ---------------------------- Geranium, cineraria, cyclamen, and many other flowering plants will do best in full sunlight, but will grow reasonably well in a southern exposure.
GROWING MEDIUM	Very porous medium ---------------------------- Most cacti and succulents require a very porous medium (one that has a large volume of perlite or sand in it). Roots of these plants tend to rot off easily in growing media that are not very porous, especially when overwatered.	Rather porous medium that drains well but holds a moderate amount of moisture	Heavy medium ---------------------------- Cyperus

Insects. The most common insect pests that bother indoor plants are aphids, whiteflies, mealybugs, scale, spider mites, fungus gnats, and springtails. Malathion, or a systemic insecticide, will normally control these pests if the directions on the label are followed. Some pesticides sold specifically for use on houseplants include pyrethrum and rotenone, which are non-toxic to humans. Malathion is relatively safe when used according to directions. Probably the safest and best method to control insects is to make sure that new plants or cuttings are free of insects before you place them with your existing plants. All of these insects can be seen easily by the naked eye, except for the spider mites.

Aphids are small sucking insects that usually *cluster* at the tips of plants where there is *new growth*. They are $\frac{1}{16}$ to $\frac{1}{8}$ inch long and feed by thrusting their beaks in among plant cells and sucking out the sap. Use malathion as directed on the label. More than one application is normally required.

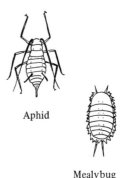

Aphid

Mealybug

Mealybugs are sucking insects slightly larger than aphids, but they cluster in leaf axils, often only one or two together. As they get larger and older, they form a cottony mass around them which hinders insecticides from killing them. Perhaps the easiest thing to do is to discard plants that are badly infested. You may manually remove mealybugs from plants if there are only a few. Then wash the plant off and perhaps spray with malathion, following the directions on the label.

Spider mites are usually found on the undersides of leaves. Where they are present, the leaves have a mottled or scurfy appearance and may be covered with thin strands like cobwebs. Use malathion or a systemic insecticide (as directed on the label) to help in their control.

Spider mite

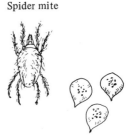

Scale are sucking insects that may bother plants indoors. The easiest way to control scale in small numbers is to wipe them off manually and watch for their return. If they keep coming back, spray with malathion as directed.

Scale

Whiteflies are small white pests about the size of fruit flies. They often congregate on the undersurfaces of leaves and will fly about when the leaves are disturbed. Use malathion repeatedly to get them under control. Insecticides are able to kill the adults, but the eggs are more difficult. They just keep on hatching, making more than one treatment necessary.

Whitefly

Fungus gnats are commonly found in growing media that contain a high proportion of organic matter, such as peat moss, especially when it is overwatered. Adults are dark brown to black and about $\frac{1}{8}$ inch long. For prevention,

Fungus gnat

Springtail

Oxalis

don't overwater plants. To control fungus gnats, use malathion as directed on the label.

Springtails are six-legged creatures about $\frac{1}{32}$ inch long and may be many different colors. They occur in moist soil and can be identified by their habit of "jumping" into the air. They can be controlled by using malathion.

Diseases. The most common disease that indoor gardeners face is *damping off*, which occurs especially on young seedlings. Seedlings develop a stem rot at the medium surface and then fall over. They may also rot before germinating. Using sterilized soil, watering early in the day, allowing air to circulate freely around seedlings, and providing adequate light all help to reduce the chances of this disease becoming a serious problem. Root rots are common when plants are overwatered. (See the section on Plant Propagation for more information.)

Weeds. A weed is commonly defined as a plant out of place, and they are a problem in the greenhouse as well as in lawns and gardens. A common weed in the greenhouse is *oxalis*. It is particularly bad because it provides a place for insects, such as whiteflies, to live, and these can reinfect other plants. Therefore, all weeds should be removed as fast as they appear, before they flower and produce seeds. The use of herbicides is not recommended.

Most Common Causes Of Indoor Plant Problems

The most common causes of indoor plant problems are listed below along with the most common effects.

Cause	Effects
Overwatering	Leaves turn yellow, leaves wilt, leaves drop off, roots rot off, plant may fall over after roots rot off, soil surface and pots may be covered with green algae, small gray-to-black flies (fungus gnats) are present in the soil and fly around when disturbed.
Low humidity	Leaf tips and leaf margins turn brown, leaves turn yellow or brown, leaves may fall off (especially the lower ones), leaves may wilt, buds may drop.
Low light	Plants tend to be tall and spindly, lower leaves drop off, flowering plants fail to produce buds or buds may fall off.

Underwatering	Leaves wilt, lower leaves drop off.
Too much light	Burned leaves (leaves tend to look grayish or bleached, especially those receiving the most light).

Diagnosing Plant Problems

To avoid most indoor plant problems:

1. Select suitable plants for the location where you plan to grow them;
2. Start with healthy plants;
3. Take special care of new plants in order to give them a chance to adjust to their new environment;
4. Water them according to their needs and do not overwater.

If you don't know what might be causing a plant problem, then you may have to consider additional causes as suggested below for each symptom.

Common Symptom	*Possible Cause(s)*
Brown or dead leaf tips and margins	Dry air, drafts, overwatering, underwatering.
Wilted leaves	Overwatering (especially if soil is soggy and has algae growing on the surface), underwatering or plant being underpotted when transpiration rates are high, high level of soluble salts.
Leaf drop	The gradual loss of lower leaves is normal for many plants. Low humidity, overwatering, over-fertilizing, drafts, changes in environment, insects.
Tall and spindly plants	Low light, temperature too warm (seedlings especially).
Yellow leaves	Too little light, lack of fertilizer (especially nitrogen), insects.
Flower and bud drop	Change in environment, low humidity.
Poor growth	Lack of fertilizer, overwatering, pot-bound, high soluble-salt level.
Yellow or brown spots on leaves	Overwatering, too much light.

ENJOYING PLANTS INDOORS

The most popular way of growing and enjoying plants indoors is by having a single plant in its own pot. Most individuals end up with many different species and sizes of plants requiring different sizes of pots. Sometimes, a few plants of the same species are planted together in one pot in order to reduce the amount of time it takes to grow a large "plant." Pots having drainage holes normally require the use of a saucer or other low container to catch any excess water draining out the bottom of the pot. Clay saucers are porous like clay pots and often are not satisfactory unless they are waxed or painted on the inside, since moisture may seep out the bottom. Clay pots are probably the most popular containers used indoors. Because they are porous, air can move through the pot to the growing medium, which usually results in better root growth. The soil of overwatered plants will also dry out more quickly in porous containers.

Individual plants can be located around rooms—near windows or light, on tables, or hung from the wall or ceiling. Several types of pot hangers are available commercially for hanging the popular sizes of pots. Plants are often grouped together on trays or shelves so that they can be cared for more easily. Grouping them together is also another way of increasing the humidity, especially if the pots are placed on a layer of gravel that is kept moist. Many indoor gardeners find it possible and easy to increase the humidity even more by covering their grouped plants with a sheet of clear plastic. This plastic sheet can be kept over the plants except when you look at them or show them.

After growing plants for a while, most indoor gardeners want to grow a collection of different plants together—in a planter, dish garden, terrarium, hanging basket, or window box. A *planter* is a container or structure in which plants in their individual pots are submerged in a medium like peat moss or vermiculite which will help keep the pots from drying out. A planter usually has a liner so that water doesn't run out the bottom. Each plant must be watered separately. Plants can be removed or changed around rather easily in a planter when they become too large or need replacing. They can even be rotated so that they don't become one-sided as they grow toward light.

It is important when selecting plants for a terrarium, dish garden, or any other grouping, that you choose plants that are *compatible*—plants that tolerate the same light, temperature, humidity, soil, and moisture conditions. It is also important to select plants that differ in size, form or shape, growth habit, texture, and color, so that the collection of plants won't look monotonous.

A small dish garden, for example, usually is made up of at least three different plants. If only foliage plants are used, one is usually an upright plant, one is often a low, spreading type, and one is a vining plant that helps tie the others together. Carefully selecting plants having leaves, stems, or flowers of different sizes, shapes, and colors will also make the dish garden more pleasing to look at.

Probably the most time-consuming task involved in the construction of dish gardens, terrariums, hanging baskets, and so on is the selection of compatible plants. Other major tasks are getting the materials together (container, plants, growing medium, etc.) and deciding where the plants are to be placed.

Dish Gardens

A dish garden is a container in which two or more plants are grown. Sometimes a dish garden is described as an uncovered terrarium, a miniature landscape, or a collection of small plants.

A good dish garden contains a collection of compatible plants growing together in a small container. Many different types of containers can be used, including pottery, glass, plastic, wood, and wicker baskets. Containers at least 3 inches deep are best because you can use a wider variety of plants and not have to worry about the container drying out so often. Containers less than 3 inches deep are especially good for small cacti and succulents. All shapes are satisfactory. Three to five plants in a small planter are sufficient.

Dish garden

Selection of Plants. There are several different types of dish gardens. Most would fall into one of the following categories: woodland, tropical, or cacti and succulents. Probably the most common type of dish garden is the one using tropical plants. Some plants which do well in dish gardens include:

Aluminum Plant	Episcia	Peperomias
Artillery Plant	False Aralia	Pepper
Asparagus Fern	Fatshedera	Philodendron
Baby's Tears	Ferns	Pick-a-Back Plant
Birdsnest Sansevieria	Grape Ivy	Pileas
Bromeliads	Hemigraphis	Plectranthus
Cacti	Jade Plant	Podocarpus
Chinese Evergreen	Kangaroo Vine	Pothos
Dracena	Nephthytis	Snake Plant
Dumbcane	Pandanus	Strawberry Begonia
English Ivy	Pellionia	Wax Plant

Excellent dish gardens can be made out of cacti and succulents such as bishop's cap, old-man's beard, peanut cactus, organ-pipe cactus, mammillaria, prickly pear cactus, bunny-ears, paper-spined opuntia, and aloe.

Growing Media. To keep plants small and keep them from outgrowing the container, use a growing medium that is not too fertile. It should be porous and well drained so that the roots have enough air.

A suitable growing medium can be made with 1 part soil, 1 part sand, and 1 part peat moss. A vermiculite and peat moss mix is also satisfactory. The growing medium should be slightly moist before planting. Make a ball of growing medium and then crumble it. If the ball does not fall apart easily, the medium is too moist.

Drainage. If the container has no drainage hole, it is usually recommended that internal drainage be provided. Drainage material may help prevent the growing medium from becoming waterlogged. Small pebbles, pieces of broken pots, coarse sand, or ground charcoal are all good drainage materials. Charcoal is especially good in that it helps keep the soil from getting smelly. Most dish gardens are not porous, since they are either glazed on the inside or made from plastic, metal, or glass. Therefore, if you have been used to growing plants in clay pots, watch out that you don't overwater the plants in a dish garden.

Procedure. Assemble the container, drainage material, growing medium, and plants on a convenient worktable. If you wish to view the dish garden from all sides, use a round or square container and place the tallest plant in the center. If the dish garden is to be viewed from only one side, place the tallest plant at one end of the container, or perhaps in the center, and place shorter plants adjacent to it. Sometimes several plants of only one species are used. Rooted cuttings can also be used.

Plants to be used should be grown in 2¼-inch or 3-inch pots so that they will fit in the dish garden without your having to break off the bottom of the soil mass. After placing drainage material in the bottom of the container, determine the position of the plants by moving them about the container until you are satisfied with their arrangement. Before doing this, remove them from the pots in which they were grown so that you can more accurately tell how they will look in the dish garden. When you have decided on the location of all the plants, fill in around the plants with the growing medium and gently firm it around the roots.

The use of figurines in most dish gardens is discouraged because figurines usually detract from plants. Likewise, the use of gaudy, highly decorated containers is discouraged—the plants should be the center of interest instead of the container. Small stones or pebbles can often be used effectively with cacti and succulents.

Add a cup or so of water at a time whenever the plants need watering. You can often tell by the weight of the garden when it is getting low on water. Never allow plants to wilt, because they often lose their bottom leaves afterwards. If they wilt, you have probably waited too long to water or you have overwatered. If the environment in which the dish garden is located is relatively constant, you may find it possible to water according to a time schedule, but this method is not nearly as good as watering when the plants need it.

Some individuals prefer to use containers having a reservoir at the base with a wick extending up into the soil mass. This method of watering is sometimes referred to as *automatic watering*.

Care. Pinch fast-growing plants often to keep them within bounds. Fertilize with a good houseplant fertilizer as directed on the label of the container. Giving the plants a shower once a month in a sink or tub will remove most dust. The use of a foliage spray is usually not desirable.

Don't expect a dish garden to last forever. If it lasts 6 months or more, you should be satisfied. Often, many of the plants in a dish garden can be reused if they are repotted. Many plants can also be propagated by cuttings which, when rooted, can be used when the dish garden is replanted.

Terrariums

A terrarium is a transparent container (usually glass) in which plants are grown. Other names for a terrarium are Wardian case, bottle garden, and glass garden. They are often used as centerpieces.

The terrarium is an excellent device for stimulating interest in plants and animals. It can be bought in various sizes and shapes. Glass aquariums, fishbowls, battery jars, brandy snifters, carboys, gallon jugs, pickle or catsup containers, and other glass jars can be used. Two clear plastic glasses taped together at their tops also are satisfactory.

Terrarium

A tight cover is sometimes used to provide high humidity so that the terrarium can function as a miniature greenhouse. If a lid is used, the terrarium can go for weeks to months without watering, but if none is used, more frequent watering will be required. Most terrariums last longer without being covered.

In addition to decoration, terrariums can be used for propagation and plant study. Cuttings can be rooted in terrariums rather easily—keep the terrarium covered until cuttings are rooted and then gradually remove the cover over a period of days.

Selection of Plants. The plants used in terrariums usually are of one or two types—woodland or tropical. The kind of terrarium you make, therefore, depends on the plants available. Plants requiring high humidity, such as fittonia and ferns, grow especially well. Some plants that can be used are listed below:

Tropical Plants

African Violet	Echeveria	Philodendron
Artillery Plant	Episcia	Pilea
Baby's Tears	Ferns	Strawberry Begonia
Chinese Evergreen	Fittonia	Streptocarpus
Creeping Fig	Maranta	Telanthera
Croton	Peperomia	Wax Begonia
Dracena		

Woodland Plants

Boxwood	Partridgeberry
Club Moss	Seedling Evergreens
Ferns	Selaginella
Hepatica	Shelf Fungus
Lichens	Violets
Liverworts	Wild Strawberry
Mosses	Wintergreen

Growing Media and Drainage. Growing media and drainage requirements are similar to those described in the section on Dish Gardens.

Procedure. Assemble the container (make sure it is clean), drainage material, growing medium, and plants on a convenient worktable. If you wish to see the terrarium from all sides, put the taller plants in the center and the smaller ones around the outside. If the terrarium will be viewed from one side only, slope the soil upward toward the back of the container and use the larger plants in back and the small ones in front.

Before planting, arrange the plants either inside or outside of the terrarium in a pleasing design. This will require more time than the actual planting. An incline can be made out of a couple of narrow stakes or wires to slide plants down inside a bottle if the neck is too narrow to reach through.

Depending on the size of the container, put ½ to 1 inch of drainage material in the flat bottom part of the container (if you decide to use drainage material). Do not slope the material up the sides of the container. With your fingers, scoop out holes large enough for the root system. Set the plants in and gently firm the growing medium around the roots. If necessary, prune back large plants or reduce the size of large root balls. This will need to be done in order to get most plants through the necks of bottles.

Do not crowd the plants or press them against the sides of the container. Do not worry about roots that are exposed, since they will not dry out in the humid atmosphere. Eventually they will work themselves into the soil.

Exposed soil may be covered with small rocks, pebbles, or moss. A small figurine, a piece of shelf fungus, or a lichen-covered rock may be added as an additional focal point. Plants are usually interesting enough by themselves so that accessories are not necessary. The surface of the growing medium will be less conspicuous if you lower it next to the glass by firming it down with your fingertips.

Watering. After planting, moisten the growing medium lightly with a mister or sprayer. The medium should be moist, but not soggy. Spray off any particles adhering to the leaves or walls of the container. The use of rain or distilled water will reduce the amount of crusting that occurs on the inside of the container at the soil level.

Finally, clean the glass with a paper tissue and put on the cover if you plan to use one. Since some ventilation is necessary to prevent condensation of moisture on the inside of the container, the cover need not fit tightly. Adjust the cover so there always is a small opening for air movement. You can make a cover out of plastic held with tape or have one made by your local glass cutter. Containers such as goblets, jars, and brandy snifters can be covered with petri dishes.

Care. Keep the terrarium in bright light, but not direct sunlight. A north or northeast window is a good location. The woodland terrarium should be kept in a cooler room than that in which the tropical terrarium is kept.

To determine if water is needed, tilt the terrarium and see if there is any water standing in the bottom. If there is, it will run up the side of the terrarium; additional water will not be needed. Often you can tell if water is needed by lifting the terrarium and feeling if it is heavy or light. Also, wet or moist growing media are darker in color than dry media. If you overwater the terrarium, leave the top off for a few days until it dries out sufficiently or use a gravy baster to remove excess water. Paper towels or a sponge can also absorb excess water.

Don't expect a terrarium to last forever. The selection of slow-growing, compatible plants will result in a terrarium that will probably last longer than one in which the plants are not carefully selected. When a terrarium is no longer pleasing to look at, replant it.

Hanging basket

Hanging Baskets

The use of hanging baskets or pots to decorate indoor gardens, terraces, patios, and greenhouses is a long-popular idea. These eye-level gardens often save valuable space and provide a profusion of flowers and foliage.

Selection of Plants. The selection of plants for a hanging basket depends mainly upon the location: indoors or outdoors, sun or shade, warm or cool temperatures. Most baskets include two species of plants—one rather upright in the center of the basket and the other trailing around the edge of the basket. When two or more species are used, make sure that they have similar cultural requirements.

Usually several rooted cuttings or small plants are used, perhaps one to three for the center and several trailers for the edge. The number of plants depends mainly on their size and the size of the basket. Select trailing types whenever possible for the best results. All the plants included in the following lists are either trailing or spreading plants except the dwarf marigolds.

Plants for Shade

Arabian Wax Cissus	German Ivy	Pilea
Artillery Plant	Grape Ivy	Plectranthus
Baby Smilax	Hemigraphis	Pothos
Baby's Tears	Impatiens	Purple Heart
Boston Fern	Kangaroo Vine	Strawberry Begonia
Browallia	Kenilworth Ivy	Streptocarpus
Callisia	Nephthytis	Tahitian Bridal Veil
Christmas Cactus	Pansy	Tradescantias
Coleus	Pellionia	Tuberous Begonia
Creeping Fig	Pepper (Piper)	Viola
English Ivy	Periwinkle	Wandering Jew
Episcia	Philodendron	Wax Begonia
Fuchsia	Pick-a-Back-Plant	

Plants for Bright Light

Asparagus Fern	Morning Glory	String of Hearts
Cherry Tomato	Nasturtium	Sweet Potato
Chlorophytum	Petunia	Telanthera
Coleus	Portulaca	Trailing Lantana
Dwarf Marigold	Sprenger Asparagus	Wax Begonia
Ivy Geranium	Strawberry Begonia	Wax Plant

Growing Media and Drainage. Soil and drainage requirements are similar to those described in the section on Dish Gardens.

Procedure. Assemble the materials for an 8- or 10-inch pot. Use about three trailing plants around the outside of the container and one to three plants in the center. The plants around the outside are sometimes slanted so that the tops project out beyond the rim. You may use either shade plants or sun-loving plants for the hanging basket.

Containers. Possible containers include clay, plastic, or metal pots, wicker containers, small tubs, and anything else that can be hung from the ceiling or a wall bracket. Metal hangers can be purchased for use with medium-sized clay pots.

Watering. After planting, moisten the growing medium thoroughly. Most hanging baskets will dry out quickly outdoors on hot, sunny, breezy days when the relative humidity is low. On such days, they may have to be watered *more* than once. Keeping plants from drying out is probably the biggest challenge when growing them in a hanging basket out-of-doors. Lining porous containers with plastic will help keep the soil from drying out. Be sure to punch a hole in the bottom for drainage if the container is to be outside.

Care. Pinch plants if necessary, and remove old flowers and seed pods. Some plants benefit if they are cut back occasionally. A good time to do this is late July or early August if you want showy baskets through the fall. Fertilizing according to the directions on a houseplant fertilizer label may be helpful. If the plants in hanging baskets used out-of-doors have all been killed by frost, take the container down, clean it out, and store it. Plastic containers may break if left out in freezing temperatures.

Forcing Branches and Bulbs

Forcing means to bring a plant into bloom ahead of its normal flowering period outdoors. Doing this in winter months can be a very rewarding experience. Winter in northern areas often tends to become rather dreary, and brightening the indoors with flowering branches and bulbs helps make these cold months more bearable. Perhaps they serve as harbingers of spring.

Forcing Flowering Branches. This procedure is very simple. Just follow these suggestions:

1. On or after the first of January, collect branches from flowering trees and shrubs such as forsythia, flowering quince, fruit trees, maples, hickories, and willow. Be sure that flower buds are present (they are larger than leaf buds). Try to collect branches when the temperature is above freezing and without ruining the shrub or tree. Branches should be 1½ to 3 feet or more in length.
2. Bring branches indoors and place the base of the stems in a bucket of water.
3. Place the bucket in a well-lighted location having a temperature of about 60°F.

4. Syringe the buds with water as they start to open to help raise the humidity.

5. Start using the branches for decoration as soon as buds begin to show color. Be sure that the base of each stem is always in water.

6. Place the branches in a cool location at night (40°F or so) and when they are not being used; this will double or triple the length of time that the flowers will last.

7. Discard the branches after the flowers fade and fall off.

Forcing Bulbs. In general, the forcing of bulbs can be broken into two different procedures which depend on the type of bulb.

Hardy bulbs such as tulips, daffodils, hyacinths, and crocus need to be potted up in the fall and subjected to cold temperatures (about 40°F) for several weeks (13 to 14), during which time they develop an extensive root system. This system is needed to support the top growth which will develop as soon as the bulbs are brought into a warm room (55° to 65°F).

Hardy bulbs can be planted outdoors during late summer if you don't want to throw the bulbs away after flowering. Just allow the foliage to continue growing for a few weeks after the flowering period is over, and then gradually withhold water until the foliage turns yellow. After the leaves have dried up, they can be broken off at soil level and the pot stored in a dry location (such as a garage or basement) until late summer when the bulbs can be planted outdoors in a flower bed or border. They should not be forced again.

Hyacinths are sometimes forced in water. The usual procedure is to fill the jar with water to the base of the bulb without actually touching it. Then the jar is placed in a cool, dark location for several weeks while roots form. When the top grows to be about 1½ inches high, the jar can be brought into a warmer room where there is bright light. If the lower flower buds start to open before the stem elongates, place the jar back in the dark until the stem elongates and then return it to a lighted room.

Tender bulbs such as paper-white narcissus and amaryllis usually can be potted up and placed on a windowsill in a warm room (60° to 70°F). They will develop roots and shoots and should flower in just a few weeks.

Paper-white narcissus will not overwinter successfully in northern climates. They are usually discarded after flowering since they cannot be forced again. Amaryllis bulbs can be forced over and over and probably the easiest method is to keep them growing constantly and let them flower at will, usually once or twice a year. Amaryllis bulbs need to be pot-bound, so grow them in a pot that is only 2 inches greater in diameter than the bulb. If amaryllis flowers are hand-pollinated and fruiting occurs, it may be possible to raise seedlings from the seeds. After the fruit matures and starts to open, cut it off and remove the seeds. Let them dry for about a day and then plant them in a regular growing medium. The seeds germinate quickly, but it will take about three years before the bulbs will be large enough to flower.

Garbage-Can Horticulture

Garbage-can horticulture

This topic could also be called "Indoor Gardening without a Budget," since it deals with plants or plant parts that are commonly discarded. Many of them can serve as the basis for inexpensive plant projects which are very interesting and educational. Only a few examples are given below.

Pineapple Top. Pineapple tops are easy to grow so don't throw them out. The best procedure is to *twist* the top off the fruit, remove about ½ inch of the lower leaves from the stem (this often exposes roots) and then place the top in perlite or sand and cover with a plastic bag. Water the propagating medium and after new roots have started to form or the existing ones have started to grow, pot the top up in a rather porous growing medium and water it in. Damaged leaves can be trimmed with shears or removed. If your plant doesn't flower after almost 2 years, put it in a plastic bag with a ripe apple for 3 days (make sure the bag is closed tightly). The apple will give off ethylene, which may induce the pineapple to flower.

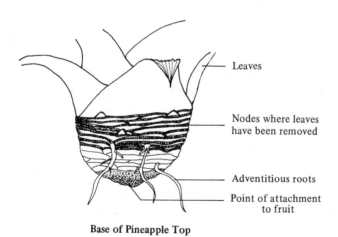

Base of Pineapple Top

Seeds. Seedling plants can be grown rather easily from the following.

To start an *avocado*, remove the thin skin around the pit, place broad end down, and half cover with growing medium. Water initially and then at weekly intervals. Covering with a plastic bag will speed germination. A new shoot will start to show in about 6 weeks. When the tree gets too large or the leaves become unattractive, either throw it out and start over or cut it back to the pit and hope that it will send up another shoot. Planting the pit upside down sometimes results in a forest of trees instead of just one stem.

White-oak *acorns* will germinate in the fall immediately when they drop off. Acorns of other oaks normally need a cold treatment (*stratification*) before they will germinate. To stratify, just place good sound acorns in a plastic bag along with some slightly moistened sand or vermiculite; close the bag and place it in a refrigerator or other cool place. After 3 to 4 months, or when they start to germinate, remove them and pot them up.

Seeds of other common horticultural plants that germinate easily include pine, nuts, honey locust, Kentucky coffee tree, asparagus, rhubarb, amaryllis, and herbs. Seeds of many woody plants need to be stratified, so if you try to germinate them and don't have any results after a few weeks, you may need to give them a cold treatment.

Woodland Plants. Mosses, fungi, violets, and many others not on protected lists make good terrarium additions.

Bedding Plants. Wax begonias, coleus, impatiens, and geraniums, which will be killed by freezing temperatures, can be rescued before frost. Just dig them up and place one plant in a 6-inch pot, cut back the tops severely (to about one-third of their original height), fertilize them with a houseplant fertilizer, and place them in as much light as possible. These plants can even be placed outdoors again the following spring when danger of frost is past. Tops removed when pruning back can also be rooted in a propagating medium. Wax begonia is especially easy to handle this way.

Cuttings. Many indoor plants can be propagated by cuttings. Examples of common, easily propagated plants which are often overlooked include the snake plant, the jade plant, peperomias, the Christmas cactus, and other cacti and succulents. For more information, see the section on Plant Propagation.

Spores. Many indoor gardeners grow ferns which reproduce by spores. Although this is a relatively slow process, it is possible to produce plants large enough for use in a terrarium in about 6 months. See the section on Plant Propagation for more information.

Coconut Shells. A very attractive hanging basket or pot can be made from a coconut shell with or without the husk. Just saw off the top and remove the meat. Holes can be drilled in the top for attaching a hanger if necessary, but simple hangers can be made or purchased that don't require holes.

Propagating or increasing plants by cuttings (slips), seeds, spores, layering, and other methods is a very interesting process. In fact, this is the area of horticulture that is the most appealing to many plant growers. The ability to produce one, two, ten, a hundred, or even thousands of new plants from just a single plant is very challenging, and once you start propagating plants and learning new methods and techniques, you have found a hobby that can be extremely satisfying.

Plant propagation is usually divided into two broad areas—non-vegetative or sexual (seeds), and vegetative or asexual (spores, cuttings, layers, grafting, and others). Examples and descriptions of the various methods of plant propagation are given below.

I. *Non-vegetative (Sexual) Propagation*

A. Seeds

1. Seed Germination

Seeds need moisture, warmth, oxygen, and in some instances light, in order to germinate. Unless special effort is taken to save seeds from one year to the next, most indoor gardeners will do best to buy fresh seeds each year from a reliable mail-order seed company that specializes in the kinds of plants that they want to grow. The main advantage of buying through a catalog is that seeds of many more varieties of plants are offered, compared with those available locally. Also, seed catalogs contain a wealth of information about plants and their culture which cannot be placed on seed packets because of limited space. Names and addresses of mail-order seed companies can be found in garden magazines.

2. Sowing Procedure

Follow the directions on the seed packet. Seeds can be germinated in small plastic trays, pots, or other relatively shallow containers filled with a mixture of vermiculite and peat moss or any medium especially recommended for seed propagation. Most artificial mixes are essentially sterile, and if they are not contaminated with garden soil or other materials, the so-called damping-off diseases which kill seedlings may be avoided.

Fill the container with the medium and gently press it down. If seeds are to be sown in rows (drills), mark them. (Wooden pot labels work well.) If seeds are to be sown at random (broadcast), then no marking is necessary.

Try to space the seeds evenly by gently shaking the seed packet. Be thrifty, especially when sowing small seeds, since every seed has the potential to germinate. If only a few plants are desired, then sow only a half-dozen or a dozen seeds. Check the seed packet to see what the germination percentage is and how many seeds are in the packet. This information (if present) will help you decide what portion of the packet you should sow.

After sowing, cover the seeds with the growing medium as directed on the packet. A general rule of thumb is to cover seeds one to three times as deep as their greatest diameter. Very fine seeds should barely be covered.

Place a label with the date and kind and variety of seeds sown in the tray. If more than one kind or variety is planted in a tray, it is recommended that seeds be sown in rows and that each row be labeled.

Moisten the surface of the medium carefully. Subirrigation is safest, and has the advantage that seeds do not get washed away. The entire container can be placed in a sink so that water will enter from below. If you water from above, use a small sprayer or mister and gently syringe the soil until water runs out the bottom of the tray. Care must be taken to keep the seeds from washing away.

Place the tray in a plastic bag or cover the tray with clear plastic or glass to provide high humidity and to reduce desiccation. Do not let the surface of the medium dry out, but if the tray is kept covered you should not have to water again until the seeds germinate.

Place the container where the temperature is 65° to 85°F. Check the seed packet for more specific information to see if light is required for germination. Don't place or leave them in full sun when covered, since the temperature may rise to levels detrimental for seedlings.

As soon as most of the seeds germinate, remove the plastic bag or cover and move the tray to a cooler location where the seedlings will receive lots of light. Seedlings grown at warm temperatures and/or in weak light become tall and spindly and are poor plants.

Transplant seedlings to small individual containers as soon as they can be handled easily (usually when the first true leaves are fully expanded). It is best to hold the seedlings by the leaves or cotyledons to avoid damaging the vascular tissues within the stem. Never pull the seedlings out of the medium, but lift or pry them out with a small stick or pencil. If the roots are well developed, the tray can be held upside down in one hand and the entire "soilblock" removed from the tray. It is normally easier to separate the seedlings without the tray. Keep as much of the root system as possible. Transplant one seedling per pot (using the smallest pots available) or per cell if transplanting to containers made up of several cells that are attached to each other. Have the pots or containers filled with growing medium which has been firmed down. (The surface should be about a half inch below the top of the pot or container.) A hole large enough for the roots should be made in the center of the pot or cell with a pointed wooden stake, pencil, or stick (dibber). Holding the seedling by the leaves or cotyledons with your thumb and forefinger, place the roots in the hole a little deeper than they were previously, and firm the medium around the roots and stem. Spindly seedlings should be set deeper than stocky seedlings. Water the seedlings promptly and place them in a shaded location while they are recovering from the shock of transplanting.

If you just want to watch seeds germinate or do a simple germination check, place the seeds on a moistened paper towel in a saucer or plastic container and place the container in a warm location. Some seeds will start to wrinkle and swell up within an hour if warm water is used.

Note the difference in germinating patterns of the seedlings. Some seedlings will push their cotyledons above the soil level while others will not. Note also the size and shape of the cotyledons: some are fleshy, divided or lobed. All have in common their total difference from the so-called true leaves. Cotyledons are sometimes referred to as seed leaves. Germination where the cotyledons emerge above ground due to the elongation of the hypocotyl is termed *epigeous*. Germination is termed *hypogeous* when the hypocotyl does not elongate and the cotyledons remain below ground.

3. Dormancy

At certain times, many seeds will not germinate even when all environmental conditions are satisfactory. This is because the seed is *dormant*—internal conditions are preventing germination. It must go through a period of rest or *dormancy* before it will germinate. Seeds purchased in stores or through mail-order companies, which will germinate when given the proper environmental conditions, are said to be *quiescent* (germination in this case being limited only by an external factor).

Dormancy is one of nature's ways of making sure that a certain kind of plant will survive. It prevents seeds from germinating during cold winters when the freezing temperatures would kill the seedlings, and it prevents all the seeds of one kind of plant from germinating in the same year. In this way, if something happens to prevent plants from producing seeds one year, such as a forest fire destroying all the plants, there are still some seeds in the soil. These seeds will sprout in the years following, and will grow into plants to replace those destroyed in the fire.

4. Why Doesn't It Sprout?

Dormancy as a result of seed-coat effects is termed *physical dormancy*. If the seed coat is water resistant, no water can pass through the seed coat to reach the embryo and the seed can't germinate. Seed coats of clover, alfalfa, honey locust and black locust seeds prevent water from reaching the embryos. Some coats prevent oxygen from reaching the embryo, which also keeps the embryo from growing; oats sometimes have this kind of seed. Sometimes the seed coat is just too strong and thick for the embryo to break out through it. Examples of this type of seed are pigweed, shepherd's purse, and peppergrass—all common weeds.

Dormancy as a result of the internal chemistry of the seed is known as *physiological dormancy*. The embryo may not be fully developed, or chemical changes must take place in the embryo or in the stored food before the seed will germinate. Seeds having this type of dormancy are apple, peach, hawthorne, basswood, ash, tulip tree, dogwood, hemlock, and pine. Tomatoes show another type of dormancy: a chemical in the tomato fruit prevents the seeds from germinating.

5. Overcoming Dormancy

Many kinds of seeds show some type of dormancy. Nature has provided this safety measure to make sure the plants will survive. Man may wish to overcome it so that he can plant the seeds and have them germinate right away. There are several ways to get them to sprout. Those processes which remove physical dormancy by altering the seed coat are known as *scarification* and result in faster and more uniform germination. Seed coats can be scratched or broken. This will weaken the seed coat so that water and oxygen can pass through and the embryo can break out. Another way to soften hard seed coats is to soak seeds in hot water for several hours, or in sulfuric acid.

A common way of overcoming dormancy caused by the embryo is by storing seeds in a cool place for several weeks. This is similar to leaving seeds on top of the ground covered with leaves and snow over winter. Seeds can be placed in a plastic bag containing moist sand, peat moss, or vermiculite and then kept at a cool temperature of 40°F for 1 to 4 months. This is about the temperature that you would find inside a refrigerator. This cool and moist storage of seeds to overcome physiological dormancy is known as *stratification*.

6. Seed Longevity

The life span, or longevity, of seeds varies from a few weeks to several hundred years, depending upon the kind of plant and how it is stored. Lotus seeds which were judged to be at least 800 years old were found recently in northern China. When planted, the seeds still grew. They were *viable* seeds, meaning that they were still able to germinate. Seeds of most of our cultivated crops rarely remain viable for more than 20 years. Seeds that are stored in a cool, dry place will live the longest. Dry ones may be kept in a screw-top jar in a home refrigerator. Most gardeners buy new seeds every year in order to be sure that the seeds will germinate.

7. Some 90-Year-Old Seeds

Over 90 years ago, William J. Beal, professor of botany and horticulture at Michigan Agricultural College (now Michigan State University), wanted to know about seed longevity. In 1879, Dr. Beal mixed seeds of 23 kinds of plants (mostly weeds) with moderately moist sand. He placed the mixture of seeds and sand in 20 pint bottles and then buried them about 20 inches deep in the ground. The mouths of the bottles slanted downward to prevent water from filling the uncorked bottles. The bottles were buried near Beaumont Tower on the campus of what is now Michigan State University in East Lansing. After 50 years, seeds of 5 kinds of plants still germinated.

In April 1970, 90 years after the experiment was started, the thirteenth bottle was dug up and the seeds were planted. Seeds of only one kind of plant germinated—those of moth mullein, a common weed.

8. Damping-off Diseases

Several fungi (*Rhizoctonia, Pythium, Phytophthora*) are responsible for the so-called damping-off diseases. Seedlings may germinate without apparent trouble, then suddenly fall over; close observation shows that the seedlings have rotted off at the soil level. Gradually all seedlings are affected throughout the whole tray. The use of non-sterilized soil is a probable cause of this.

If sterilized soil or propagating medium is obtained, care should be taken not to infest it again. This can be accomplished by maintaining the worktable free from contaminated soil (e.g., soil from outdoors), by not placing objects (pails, pots, etc.) on the table which were on the floor, and by not sitting on the table (soil particles could adhere to clothes and shoes). Work benches and tables should be sterilized prior to use with disinfectant such as chlorox. Use a 10% solution, 1 part chlorox in 9 parts water. This also may be used for soaking and cleaning pots.

Sterilized soil can be prepared by steaming (a procedure too elaborate for homeowners), pouring hot water over the soil (rather messy), treating the soil with a chemical (often hard to find), or baking in an oven at 300°F for about 45 minutes (the time required to bake a medium-sized potato). If the baking method is used, the soil should be moist. Soil needs to be at 180°F for 30 minutes to kill most of the unwanted organisms. Place moist soil in a shallow pie pan, cover with aluminum foil, and place a cooking thermometer through the foil into the center of the soil. Since some organisms will not be killed by 180°F, this treatment should be referred to as "pasteurization" rather than "sterilization."

A growing medium of vermiculite and peat moss with fertilizer added to it has proven to be satisfactory for growing plants. This artificial mix is essentially sterile and can be easily obtained.

Some damping-off diseases, so-called water molds, occur especially under moist and cool conditions. By growing the seedlings in a drier and warmer place, the spread can be prevented. Temporary suppression is possible, but the diseases can hardly be eliminated. Suppression of the spread can be achieved by:

a. Covering the tray with a layer of milled sphagnum moss (contains fungi-statics) or a layer of fine sand.
b. Reducing the watering.
c. Watering only in the morning.
d. Increasing the movement of air around the seedlings.
e. Reducing the humidity around the seedlings.
f. Using soil drenches such as Terraclor, Morsodren, and Panodrench.

PARTIAL LIST OF PLANTS
COMMONLY PROPAGATED BY SEEDS

Baby Smilax *(Asparagus asparagoides)*	4,000 seeds/oz. Germination is enhanced when seeds are placed in the dark, so cover seeds. Seeds germinate slowly (about 30 days) and lose viability rapidly, so freshly harvested seeds should be used.
Cactus	Seeds often come as a mixture of various types and species. Seeds usually germinate in 2 to 4 weeks. Use rather porous propagation medium and don't overwater.

Coleus	100,000 seeds/oz. Seeds are small to handle and need light for germination. Germination in 10 days.
Cyperus	Seeds germinate easily and quickly if kept moist. Seeds are quite inexpensive and plants can be grown easily if not allowed to dry out.
Freckleface (Hypoestes)	Germinates easily. Plants should be pinched rather frequently.
Herbs	Many common herbs germinate easily. Chives, sage, lavender, borage, basil, lemon balm, and many others.
Honey Locust	Shade tree with fine, feathery leaves. Long pods in fall and winter. Seeds germinate fast and do not need a cold treatment. Plant seedlings out-of-doors after danger of frost is past.
Kenilworth Ivy	Small, creeping plant with snapdragon-like flowers.
Marigolds	The small, short varieties can be grown successfully indoors. About 9,000 seeds/oz. They germinate quickly (within a week). Lay seeds flat on soil and cover slightly.
Nephthytis	Seeds germinate rather slowly so patience is needed. Small plants are particularly nice for dish gardens before they start trailing all over.
Norfolk Island Pine	Fresh seeds germinate rather easily if they can be obtained in late summer.
Oak	White-oak acorns germinate immediately after they fall from the tree. Plant acorns with root pointed down in soil. Nice small trees.
Pine	Seeds can be collected from cones used in dried arrangements or from trees (including Christmas). Seeds from many species exhibit dormancy which may be overcome by subjecting them to a cool temperature (about 40°F) for about 30 to 90 days. Mix seeds with

slightly moist sand or vermiculite before this treatment to keep them from drying out.

Schefflera	Seeds germinate rather slowly. Small plants can be used in dish gardens.
Sensitive Plant (Mimosa pudica)	Interesting pot plants when small, become rather shrubby when older, but can be easily resown. Sometimes plant produces flowers and seeds. Seeds germinate within a week. Cover seeds. 4,500 seeds/oz.
Sprenger Asparagus	Seeds take up to a month to germinate. Seedlings grow into very desirable plants. This is the most common asparagus grown indoors.

II. *Vegetative (Asexual) Propagation*

A. Spores

Fern spores can be started on a small clay pot (turned upside down) or on a compressed peat pot. Take a small container filled with water and place the upturned pot or peat pellet in the water. After the pot is moist on top (you can soak it), sprinkle fern spores on its top and sides. Then cover it with a clear plastic dome, glass, or other transparent container and place it where it will receive bright light. Be sure that there is water in the bottom of the container so that the pot will not dry out.

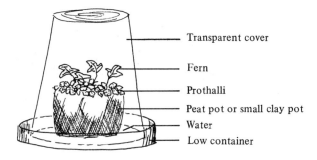

Transparent cover

Fern

Prothalli

Peat pot or small clay pot
Water
Low container

Spores are usually collected by placing a newspaper underneath a fern and shaking or tapping the fern fronds. Spores which are produced in *sporangia* on the undersides, tips, or edges of the fronds will drop out on the newspaper. They are small, so you must be very careful. Fold the newspaper in half and funnel the spores into a small envelope.

Another method of collecting spores is to cut off a fern frond as the sporangia are forming, while they are light green. Then place the frond in an envelope for several days until the sporangia mature and open up to shed spores—at this stage sporangia become darker in color.

If a fern had spores that were being shed at the time you attempted to collect them, the pot should turn green within 6 weeks after shaking spores onto it. A few weeks later, small ferns may be seen growing out of small, horizontal green structures called *prothalli* (*prothallus* is the name for a single structure). Spores of algae may have contaminated the pot or peat pellet and may also be germinating.

B. Cuttings

A cutting is any vegetative part of a plant which is capable of regenerating the missing plant parts when removed from the parent. Cuttings normally are identical with the parent. The use of rooting hormones will be beneficial on cuttings of plants that normally root slowly or are hard to root. The time and effort of using hormones on most indoor plants is probably not justified since most of them will normally root within 1 to 2 weeks. When used on indoor plants, the lower concentrations (1,000 to 3,000 ppm of IBA) are sufficient. The cut ends of cuttings are dipped in the powder and the excess removed before placing them in the propagating medium.

1. Root Cuttings (chrysanthemum, apple, cherry, hawthorn, flowering quince, plum, pear).

Take root cuttings 1 to 3 inches long. Keep the end that grew closest to the parent plant up. Roots of fruit trees ¼ to ½ inch in diameter are best. Place in coarse sand, vermiculite, or peat moss in a vertical position with the top just barely out of the rooting medium.

2. Stem Tip Cuttings (geranium, coleus, chrysanthemum, peperomia, wax begonia, lilac, forsythia).

The following simplified procedure is commonly used for taking stem tip cuttings:

a. Cut 2 to 5 inches from the tip.
b. Remove bottom leaves that would be covered by the rooting medium.
c. Place cuttings in medium in a tray or pot.
d. Place container in a clear plastic bag.
e. Place in diffused light at 55° to 75°F.
f. Remove from bag or open bag after a few days.

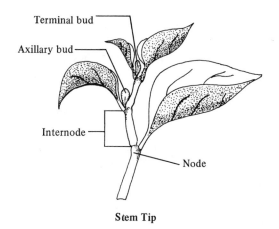

Terminal bud

Axillary bud

Internode

Node

Stem Tip

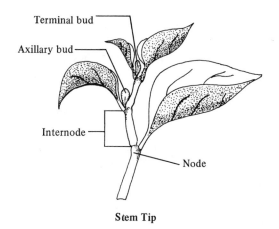

Since the most common method of propagating plants vegetatively is by stem tip cuttings, a more complete procedure is given here for those indoor gardeners who are either inexperienced in propagating plants or who are having poor results.

a. Select healthy stock plants that are free from insects.

b. Cut or pinch stem tips 2 to 5 inches either just below or just above a node. If you cut just below a node, you may be leaving an internode on the stock plant that will be unsightly and which should be cut to just above the top node. If you cut just above a node, the internode remains as part of the cutting and should be removed before sticking the cutting in the rooting medium.

c. Remove the lower leaf or leaves from nodes that will be covered by the rooting medium. You usually can just strip them off.

d. If a rooting hormone is used, dip the basal end of the cuttings into the powder and remove the excess by gently tapping the end or by touching or rubbing the end against the side of the container.

e. Insert the basal end of the cutting into the rooting medium so that at least one node is covered. This is important since roots form at nodes. Coarse sand, vermiculite, and perlite are the media most often used alone. Peat moss is sometimes added to sand and perlite to increase their moisture retention capabilities. Mixtures of 4 parts sand or perlite to 1 part peat make good media for propagating most houseplants.

f. Firm medium around cuttings if the medium is very loose. This usually is accomplished by watering as described in the next step.

g. Moisten medium slowly without washing it away from cuttings, until water runs out the bottom of the medium. Vermiculite will probably have to be watered more than once since it holds so much water and won't become saturated by just one watering.

h. Cover the cuttings with clear plastic or glass, place in a plastic bag or transparent container, or place under mist until rooted. It usually takes one to several weeks for rooting to occur. The species of plant, temperature of rooting medium, and time of year are the primary factors that affect the time required for rooting.

i. Cuttings should be placed in a well-lighted area (preferably not direct sunlight) where the temperature is between 50° and 75°F. Room temperature is satisfactory for most indoor plants. Heating the rooting medium to 65° or 75°F by use of a heating cable may reduce the time required for rooting.

j. After a few days, cuttings should be exposed to drier air by gradually opening the plastic bag or cover (hardening off).

k. Cuttings can be checked for root development after a week by gently lifting (not pulling) each cutting out of the rooting medium. This is done by inserting a wooden stake, pen, pencil, or knife under the base of the cutting and lifting the cutting up. If sufficient roots have formed in comparison with the shoot (leaves and stem), then the cutting may be potted up in a suitable soil mix. Make sure that the particles of rooting medium that are being held by the roots are not removed. Most cuttings are placed in the smallest size of pot that will hold the root system, normally a 2- or 2¼-inch pot. If no roots have formed, or there are not enough for potting, then carefully insert the cutting back into the medium. (You may have to make a hole in the medium with a pencil or knife so that you won't break off the roots). Gently pack the medium around the cutting and/or water the cutting. Check for roots again in a week.

l. Cuttings are potted up by placing a small amount of growing medium in the bottom of the pot, setting the rooted cutting in the pot, and covering the roots with the medium. Gently firm the medium around the roots. Make sure that the growing medium level is just at the base of the rim located at the top of the pot so that there will be a reservoir for water. Be sure to water cuttings promptly so that they don't wilt. Potting up cuttings late in the afternoon will allow them to recover overnight before being exposed to bright light. If they wilt severely, they can be placed back in a plastic bag until they become turgid again, and then they can be exposed gradually to the harsh environment of a room.

m. Once cuttings have become established in pots, you will need to be concerned with the following:

(1) Fertilizing. Fertilize once a week, every other week, or monthly, depending on the recommendation on the fertilizer container and the plant's requirements.

(2) Pinching.

(3) Repotting. Repot into the next larger pot when the plant outgrows the one that it is in. If roots become pot-bound, or the plant dries out very quickly, then it should be repotted. A plant is pot-bound when the roots are so closely packed that there is little room left for further growth. This condition is most easily determined by knocking the soil mass out of the pot.

3. Leaf Bud Cuttings (rubber plant, fatshedera).

This method is very similar to stem cuttings, but only one axillary bud and a short piece of the stem are included. This method is commonly used in place of regular stem cuttings when the propagation material is in short supply. Adventitious roots emerge from the stem and the bud eventually develops into the shoot.

4. Leaf Petiole or Whole-Leaf Cuttings (African violet, jade plant, peperomia, rex begonia).

a. Very similar to leaf bud cuttings.

b. Use a medium-sized young leaf with a petiole preferably about 1 inch long. Don't use very old, large leaves or very young, small leaves.

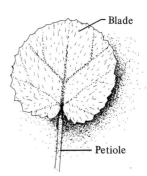

Blade

Petiole

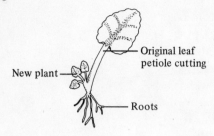

New plant — Original leaf petiole cutting

— Roots

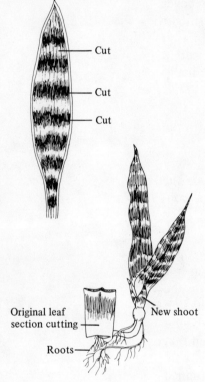

— Cut

— Cut

— Cut

Original leaf section cutting —

New shoot

Roots —

c. Remove a leaf from the parent plant by cutting the petiole.

d. Insert leaf into medium enough to cover petiole. Firm medium around petiole and moisten medium. Follow directions for stem tip cuttings. Adventitious roots arise from the petiole as does a new shoot.

5. Leaf Section Cuttings (snake plant, peperomia).

a. Take about a 2-inch section of leaf and place the *basal* end in medium. If vermiculite is used, do not firm it or keep it too moist.

b. Cuttings should neither be allowed to dry out nor be kept too moist.

c. After several weeks, roots will form.

d. After several more weeks, a new plant will form.

e. New plants can be removed from the leaf section and potted up, or the entire leaf section with roots and new plant can be potted up.

f. If the new plants are removed, the leaf section will form another new plant (snake plant).

g. Leaf section cuttings from a variegated snake plant will produce only green, non-variegated leaves because new plants are formed from the center of the leaf, which is green.

6. Stem Section Cuttings (dumbcane, dracena, Chinese evergreen).

a. Use stem sections having at least one node.

b. Place sections horizontally in sand or vermiculite.

c. Cover the bottom half of the section.

d. Pot up when rooted.

7. Viviparous Leaves (bryophyllum).

a. Some plants produce plantlets from the lobes on the leaves.

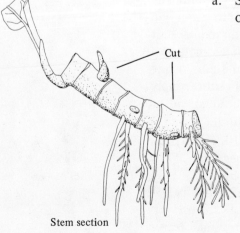

— Cut

Stem section

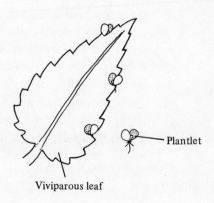

— Plantlet

Viviparous leaf

    b. These foliar embryos usually root while still attached to the leaf. Either the parent leaf or the foliar embryos then drop off and become anchored on the ground.

    c. Plantlets can be picked off and potted up in any standard growing media.

  8. Don'ts.

    a. Do not overwater cuttings. Water after you first insert them and then don't water again until the medium begins to dry out (which doesn't happen very fast in a closed plastic bag).

    b. Don't fertilize cuttings while they are rooting.

    c. Don't pull cuttings up to check for roots until at least a week after cuttings have been made.

C. Grafting (fruit trees, rose, cacti, coleus, plectranthus)

Grafting is the method of joining parts of plants together in such a way that they unite and then grow as a single plant. The top of the graft combination is called the *scion* and the part onto which the scion is grafted (lower portion) is termed the *rootstock* or *understock*, usually just referred to as *stock*. Plants need to be quite closely related taxonomically in order for grafting to be a success. A rose variety grafted onto a seedling rose, an apple variety on an apple seedling, and one coleus variety grafted onto another coleus are grafts that normally are successful. It is imperative that the cambium (cell-generating) layer of the stock be in intimate contact with the cambium of the scion. The cambium layer is the layer of meristematic cells between the xylem and phloem tissues.

There are many different grafting methods. The whip-and-tongue graft is one common method, and the cleft and splice grafts are others. For most beginners, the cleft and splice grafts will probably be easier than the whip-and-tongue method. Herbaceous plants such as cactus, geranium, and coleus are usually grafted with the cleft or splice grafts.

Indoor plants like coleus and plectranthus can be grafted by a splice graft. Select a scion that is about the same diameter as the stock and cut it off on a long, sloping slant about 1 to 2 inches long. Make the cut as smooth as possible. Cut the top of the stock to match the cut on the scion. Place the two cut surfaces together (additional cutting and fitting may be necessary) and secure them with rubber bands, tape or other materials. Place a moistened paper towel over the top of the scion and cover both the scion and graft with a transparent plastic bag which is sealed at the base. Shade the scion for a few days, and if it remains or becomes turgid, the graft has apparently taken and the plastic bag can be carefully removed. If the scion tends to wilt, cover it again with the plastic bag and then gradually expose the scion to the air. Remove the tape or rubber band after a few weeks.

Cleft grafting can be used to graft cacti. Prepare the stock by cutting it off squarely at the point you wish to graft. With a knife, split the end of the stock to a depth of an inch or so and place a wedge in it to hold it open. Use a sharp knife to trim the base of the scion so that it will end up shaped like a wedge. You may want to make the wedge a little bit thicker on one side so it fits into the stock better. Once the scion is prepared, you can insert it into the stock. When the scion is in place, (you may have to pin it), you can remove the wedge. Then the cut surfaces should be covered with a plastic bag, and shaded to protect them from overheating in direct sunlight. Leave the bag on the graft until new growth starts.

D. Budding (fruit trees)

Budding is a form of grafting in which only a small piece of wood containing a single bud is the scion. Bud grafts are made any time during the growing season when the bark of the stock will peel easily (is slipping) from the wood and dormant buds are available. Seedlings or rooted cuttings are often used as the understock. A good size of stock for budding is $3/16$ to $3/8$ inch in diameter, which is about the thickness of a pencil.

E. Division

Division is a propagation method where rhizomes, tubers, etc., are *cut apart* into sections.

1. A *rhizome* is a horizontal stem that grows at or below the surface of the ground. Rhizomes resemble roots, but differ in that they have nodes, internodes, buds, and leaves. Rhizomes may be slender, as in quack grass, or thick and fleshy, as in cannas and irises. Ferns have rhizomes, but no above-ground stem. The leaf stalk seen above the ground is a petiole. Another example is lily-of-the-valley.

2. Sometimes the growing tips of rhizomes become enlarged as a result of food storage; these structures are called *tubers*. The Irish potato is a good

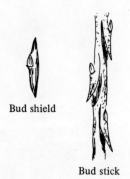

Bud shield

Bud stick

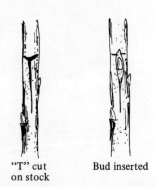

"T" cut
on stock

Bud inserted

Underground stem:
grass rhizome

example. The "eyes" of the potato are bud clusters. At each node, buds are formed in the axil of a single tiny scale-like leaf. For propagation, a tuber is cut into pieces, each with one or more "eyes."

Underground stem: potato tuber

3. Many plants are commonly propagated by *crown division*. The crown is the part of a plant at the surface of the ground that gives rise to new shoots. The proliferation of new shoots frequently leads to crowding, either in a pot or in a clump of plants in the garden. The crowded shoots are either dug up or knocked out of the pot, and they can be pulled apart or cut with a clean, sharp knife. Roots should be present on each section that is to be replanted. Potted plants can be divided whenever they become too crowded. Spring blooming garden plants are usually divided in the fall. Late summer and fall blooming garden plants are usually divided in early spring. Some plants commonly propagated by crown division include: African violet, birds-nest sansevieria, cast-iron plant, snake plant, cyperus (houseplants); and chrysanthemum, day lily, shasta daisy (garden plants).

Crown division

4. Plants having *tuberous roots* may be propagated by division. In order to grow, each section must contain a bud. It is easiest to see buds and make the proper cuts after they have begun to sprout. Dahlias and tuberous begonias are dug in the fall and stored over winter. In the spring when they begin to sprout, they can be divided. Sweet potatoes are usually propagated in special beds under warm, moist conditions. When the shoots are large and well rooted they are pulled away from the tuberous root and planted.

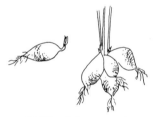

Dividing tuberous roots

5. An *offset* is a short lateral branch which develops from the crown and terminates in a rosette of leaves. Pineapple and escheveria are examples. Offsets can be cut away close to the crown and potted up in a growing medium if rooted. If not rooted, they can be handled as a cutting.

F. Separation

Separation is similar to division but involves the use of naturally occurring seams which allow the pulling apart of plant structures.

1. A *bulb* consists of a small stem at its lower end with many fleshy, scale-like leaves growing from the upper surface of the stem. Adventitious roots

emerge from the bottom of the stem. Bulbs function in food storage and vegetative reproduction. Some plants with bulbs are the onion, tulip, narcissus, lily, and hyacinth.

2. *Corms* resemble bulbs, but their structure is different. The greatest portion of the corm is stem tissue with only thin and often papery leaves. Adventitious roots grow from the lower surface of the stem. Corms also function in food storage and vegetative reproduction. Gladiolus and crocus have corms.

G. Runners (stolons)

A runner or stolon is a stem that grows horizontally along the ground (strawberry, strawberry begonia). The plants produced at the end of the runner can be rooted either by allowing them to root in place or by removing the runner and rooting it under mist or in a plastic bag. Strawberry begonia is a rather common houseplant (sometimes called strawberry geranium) which produces many runners when the humidity is quite high. Many people root these runners by placing small pots filled with a good potting soil around the entire plant and anchoring the tip of the runners to the soil in the small pots. As soon as the runners have rooted, they can be severed from the parent plant. The spider plant also sends out runners.

H. Suckers

Some plants can be propagated by means of *suckers*. A sucker is a new shoot that grows up beside the old plant. Below ground it is attached to the root system of the parent plant. Suckers are dug up and severed from the parent plant. Usually they have developed their own roots and can be potted up, but if roots have not yet formed they should be treated as cuttings until they root. Plants that can be propagated this way include cherry, apple, red raspberry, anthurium, aloe, and parlor palm.

I. Layering

This is a method of propagation in which adventitious roots develop on the stem while the stem is still attached to the parent plant. After the stem is rooted, it is then cut off and grown on its own roots. Layering is usually most successful if done in spring or late summer. Rooting is most vigorous in cool weather.

Simple layering is when a low branch is bent to the ground and covered, except for the tip. Usually

Sucker

the branch is *wounded* where it remains in the soil. One method of wounding is to cut part way through the stem on a slant about a foot below the tip and bend the top portion up at the wound. Tip layering occurs naturally on such plants as blackberries and forsythia. Tips of branches in contact with the soil root and form new shoots.

Air layering is a type of layering that is done on rubber plants and dumbcane. Usually the stem is wounded anywhere from 12 to 18 inches beneath the tip of the branch. Wounding can be done by girdling (removing a complete ring of bark), or by cutting about halfway through the stem and then propping the wound open with a toothpick or matchstick to prevent healing. Rooting hormones may be applied to the wounded area. This area then is usually wrapped with moistened sphagnum moss and covered with either clear or black plastic. The ends of the plastic are tied or taped closed in order to keep the sphagnum moss moist. Most plants require several weeks to a few months to root. When several roots have formed, the stem is cut off beneath the layer, the sphagnum moss and the plastic are removed, and the plant is potted up in a suitable growing medium.

If the only reason for air layering is to end up with a new plant that isn't leggy (such as a rubber plant), it is usually easier to cut the existing plant off at the base and force one of the axillary buds. Since the root system is already present, a new shoot will usually develop quickly. Be careful not to overwater the new shoot while it is developing.

Propagating Media

The most common media used for propagating indoor plants are sand, peat moss, vermiculite, and perlite. They are used either alone or in mixtures.

Sand is essentially small pieces of rock. Coarse or sharp sand is best for propagation purposes. It is the heaviest of all propagating media, contains practically no nutrients, and holds only a limited amount of water. It can be used alone but is often mixed with peat moss.

Peat moss consists of partially decomposed plants. It can hold a lot of water and does contain a little nitrogen. Peat is usually not used alone because of its high water-holding capacity and poor aeration. It usually is used in combination with sand or perlite. The pH of peat moss may vary considerably.

Vermiculite comes from the mineral mica, which, when heated to about 2,000°F, expands or pops like popcorn. Vermiculite is very light in weight, can absorb a lot of water, has a neutral pH, and contains essentially no nutrients except magnesium and potassium. It is often used alone for rooting cuttings, but it should not be packed down. It is also used for covering newly planted seeds. The No. 2, or horticultural grade, is most commonly used.

Perlite is a white material from volcanic rock or lava. The ore is heated to about 1,800°F to expand it. It is very light, essentially neutral, contains no nutrients, and holds three to four times its weight of water. It can be used alone, but usually is mixed with peat moss or vermiculite.

Sand and perlite are especially good for rooting plants that tend to rot off, such as cacti and succulents. Both media are very porous and dry out rather quickly.

Water sometimes is used for propagating plants. The number of species that can be rooted in water is rather limited, but includes the African violet, philodendron, geranium, impatiens, coleus, ivies, and wax plant. Some of these plants can even be grown in water for some time after they have rooted. The main disadvantage of using water is the lack of aeration. Cuttings should be potted up in a suitable growing medium before roots get too long.

Plant
identification
and culture

PLANT DESCRIPTION SYSTEM

The plants are listed alphabetically, first by family and then by common name (or genus) within a family. The classification follows that used in the second edition of A. B. Graf's *Exotic Plant Manual*. Some characteristics of each family are included as well as the approximate number of genera and species in each family.

The following outline is used in this section:

1. Family Name and Characteristics
2. Common Name
    Other Common Name(s) (listed in parentheses). The genus is often used as another common name.
    Scientific Name—Genus, Species, Cultivar (sp = species, singular; spp. = species, plural). When the name of the genus is the same as the common name, it is not spelled out again in its entirety—only the first letter is used.
    Pronunciation. The scientific name is divided syllabically for pronunciation, with the syllable which has primary stress being capitalized.
    Where the Plant Comes From
3. Common Description of the Plant
    Special Care Required, Use, etc. Most plants included in this book will grow indoors under average household conditions. Special cultural conditions are given only when necessary to insure success.
4. Common Method(s) of Propagation

Acanthaceae

1. Aphelandra
2. Fittonia
3. Freckleface (*Hypoestes*)
4. Hemigraphis
5. Shrimp Plant

Amaranthaceae

6. Iresine
7. Telanthera

Amaryllidaceae

8. Amaryllis
9. Paper-White Narcissus

Araceae

10. Anthurium
11. Chinese Evergreen
   (*Aglaonema*)
12. Dumbcane (*Dieffenbachia*)
13. Monstera
14. Nephthytis (*Syngonium*)
15. Philodendron
16. Pothos (*Scindapsus*)

Araliaceae

17. English Ivy
18. False Aralia
19. Fatshedera
20. Umbrella Tree

Araucariaceae

21. Norfolk Island Pine
   (*Araucaria*)

Asclepiadaceae

22. String of Hearts
23. Wax Plant (*Hoya*)

Balsaminaceae

24. Impatiens

Begoniaceae

25. Angel-Wing Begonia
26. Rex Begonia
27. Wax Begonia

Bromeliaceae

28. Pineapple

Cactaceae

29. Christmas Cactus
30. Opuntia

Commelinaceae

31. Callisia
32. Moses in the Cradle (*Rhoeo*)
33. Purple Heart

34. Tahitian Bridal Veil
35. Tradescantia (*T. albiflora*
   'Albo-vittata')
36. Tradescantia (*T. fluminensis*
   'Variegata')
37. Trailing Callisia
38. Wandering Jew (*Zebrina*)

Compositae

39. Chrysanthemum
40. Cineraria
41. German Ivy
42. Velvet Plant

Crassulaceae

43. Bryophyllum (*Kalanchoe*)
44. Echeveria
45. Jade Plant
46. Jelly Beans

Cyperaceae

47. Cyperus

Euphorbiaceae

48. Chenille Plant
49. Croton
50. Crown of Thorns
51. Poinsettia

Geraniaceae

52. Geranium

Gesneriaceae

53. African Violet
54. Episcia
55. Gloxinia
56. Streptocarpus

Labiatae

57. Coleus
58. Plectranthus

Leguminosae

59. Sensitive Plant (*Mimosa*)

Liliaceae

60. Aloe
61. Baby Smilax
62. Birdsnest Sansevieria
63. Cast-Iron Plant (*Aspidistra*)
64. Chlorophytum
65. Dracena (*D. fragrans*)
66. Dracena (*D. marginata*)
67. Dracena (*D. sanderiana*)
68. Easter Lily
69. Hyacinth

70. Snake Plant (*Sansevieria*)
71. Sprenger Asparagus
72. Ti Plant
73. Tulip

Malvaceae
74. Flowering Maple

Marantaceae
75. Prayer Plant (*Maranta*)

Moraceae
76. Creeping Fig
77. Fiddle-Leaf Fig
78. Rubber Plant (*Ficus*)

Onagraceae
79. Fuchsia

Orchidaceae
80. Orchid (*Cattleya*)
81. Orchid (*Cymbidium*)

Palmaceae
82. Parlor Palm

Piperaceae
83. Emerald Ripple Peperomia
84. Peperomia (*P. obtusifolia*)
85. Peperomia (*P. rubella*)
86. Pepper (*Piper*)
87. Watermelon Peperomia

Pittosporaceae
88. Pittosporum

Podocarpaceae
89. Podocarpus

Polypodiaceae
90. Boston Fern
91. Staghorn Fern
92. Table Fern

Primulaceae
93. Cyclamen

Rutaceae
94. Citrus

Saxifragaceae
95. Pick-a-Back Plant
96. Strawberry Begonia

Scrophulariaceae
97. Kenilworth Ivy

Urticaceae
98. Aluminum Plant
99. Artillery Plant
100. Baby's Tears
101. Pellionia
102. Pilea (*P. depressa*)

Vitaccae
103. Arabian Wax Cissus
104. Grape Ivy
105. Kangaroo Vine

(handwritten margin notes)

8fl group

7th group

8fl group

4th group

(right column handwritten notes)

106 Asplenium
Birdnest fern
70°
No direct sun
wet

107 Evonymus
55-60°
Filtered sun
moist

108 Aucuba
Gold Dust Tree
55-60°
Filtered sun
Drench Dry

109 Buxus
Boxwood
55-60°
Bright sun
moist

110 Adiantum
Maidenhair fern
80-85°
No direct sun
wet

DESCRIPTIONS OF SELECTED HOUSEPLANTS

Family: Acanthaceae
a canth A ce ae
Acanthus Family
Perennial armed or unarmed herbs or shrubs; leaves opposite, simple, without stipules.
Acanth = thorn.

Number of Genera: 240   Species: 2,200

1. Aphelandra (zebra plant)
   A. squarrosa
   aph e LAN dra   squarr O sa
   Brazil.
   Plant with showy leaves having white veins and showy terminal flower spikes. Does best in filtered sun. Keep the soil moist. Drops lower leaves if air or soil is too dry.

   Propagated by stem tip cuttings.

80-85° DT
Filtered sun
moist

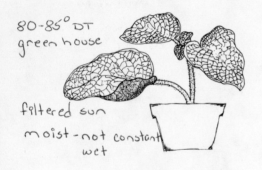

80-85° DT
green house

filtered sun

moist - not constant
wet

2. Fittonia
F. verschaffeltii
fit TO ni a   ver schaf FEL ti i
Peru.
Low, trailing plant having oval leaves which are
dark green and netted with white *veins*. Requires high humidity and therefore should be
grown in a greenhouse or terrarium. Keep
rather moist.

Propagated by stem tip cuttings.

80-85°
Filtered sun
moist

3. Freckleface (polka dot)
Hypoestes ~~sanguinolenta~~ phyllostachya
hy po ES tes   san guin o LEN ta
Madagascar.
Interesting plant because of the pink freckles
scattered in the green leaves. Does best in
bright light. Requires *frequent pinching* to
keep it compact.

Propagated by stem tip cuttings and seeds.

80-85°
No direct sun
Moist

4. Hemigraphis
H. ~~colorata~~ alternata
hem i GRAPH is   col or AT a
Java.
Creeping plant having purple to dark green
leaves and small white flowers. Prefers high
humidity and moist soil. Can be used in a
hanging basket.

Propagated by stem tip cuttings.

5. Shrimp Plant
~~*Beloperone guttata*~~ Justicia brandegeana
bel o per ON e   gut TA ta
Mexico.
An interesting plant because of the over-
lapping, *reddish-brown bracts* which partially
cover the white flowers. Does best in bright
light. Keep on the moist side and do not let the
soil dry out between waterings. Needs to be
pinched back often to keep it from becoming
tall and scraggly.

Propagated by stem tip cuttings.

Family: Amaranthaceae
am a ranth A ce ae
Amaranth Family
Plants often with highly colored foliage or
showy flower heads.
Number of Genera: 400   Species: 8,000

6. Iresine (blood leaf)
I. spp.
I re sine
Brazil.
Has rounded, opposite leaves which are notched
at the tip, or rather long leaves with pointed
tips. Foliage may be dark red or green. Needs
to be pinched often to keep from becoming
leggy. *Iresine* is Greek for 'woolly harvest
garland,' an allusion to the woolly flowers. *I.
herbstii* has purplish-red leaves with notched
leaf tips. *I. h. aureo-reticulata* has green leaves
with yellow veins. *I. lindenii* has narrow, red
leaves with pointed tips.

Propagated by stem tip cuttings.

7. Telanthera (Joseph's coat-of-many-colors)
Alternanthera spp.
al tern AN ther a
Brazil.
Low-growing foliage plants having opposite,
narrow, small leaves. Leaves may be different
shades of green and yellow *or* green, pink, and
red. Excellent for edging in flower beds.

Propagated by stem tip cuttings.

Family: Amaryllidaceae
am a ryll i DA ce ae
Amaryllis Family
Mostly tropical bulbous plants similar to
those in the lily family.
Number of Genera: 86   Species: 1,310

8. Amaryllis
Hippeastrum vittatum
hipp e AS trum vitt A tum
Peru.

Bulbous plant with large, showy flowers produced on *scapes* (leafless stems). Leaves are basal and strap-like. Bulbs are tender. Pot diameter should be 2 inches greater than the diameter of the bulb. Cover one-third to one-half of bulb with a porous soil mixture. After flowering, fertilize until fall. Then gradually withhold water, and let bulbs go dormant. In January, replace part of the top soil with fresh soil, and start watering to force the bulb. Bulbs can be forced annually for 30 or more years. See page 52 for another method.

Propagated by removing the small bulbs which form to the side of the original bulb. Can also be propagated by seeds if the flowers are pollinated, but it takes 2 to 3 years for the seedlings to grow large enough to flower.

9. Paper-White Narcissus
   Narcissus tazetta
   nar CIS sus   ta ZETT a
   Canary Islands.
   Has showy, white, fragrant flowers bunched together at the tips of the stems. Bulbs are not hardy and are usually discarded when flowering ceases or grown on for nice foliage.

   Propagated by bulbs.

Family: Araceae
   a RA ce ae
   Arum Family (Aroid or Calla Family)
   Mostly tropical plants with a bitter, sometimes poisonous juice. Flowers are small, located on a spadix with a bract, or spathe, below.
Number of Genera: 105   Species: 1,400

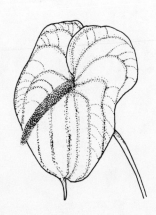

10. Anthurium
    A. scherzerianum
    an THUR i um   scher zer i A num
    Columbia.
    Erect plants with long-lobed, heart-shaped leaves grown for their colorful spathes (white, pink, red) which last several weeks. Prefers moist soil and humid air. Does best in partial shade. Use half soil and half sphagnum moss for the soil mix, and keep it moist. *A.*

andraeanum is grown in Hawaii and is known for its large, showy flowers, which are used in flower arrangements.

Propagated by division.

11. Chinese Evergreen

Aglaonema commutatum
ag la o NE ma   com mu TA tum
Southeastern China.
A very popular, durable houseplant having waxy, entire green leaves up to 10 inches long. It can be grown in water. Does best in shade or partially shaded areas and is one of the plants most tolerant of low light intensities. Keep the soil constantly moist. Many species are used as houseplants.

Propagated by division or by stem section cuttings.

12. Dumbcane
Dieffenbachia amoena
dieff en BACH i a   a MOE na
South America.
Handsome foliage plants with *sheathing petioles* and irregular light-colored or yellow markings between the pinnate veins in the leaves. Plants grow to almost 4 feet tall and prefer partial shade. Avoid contact with sap of stems, which is poisonous. Let soil *dry out* between waterings.

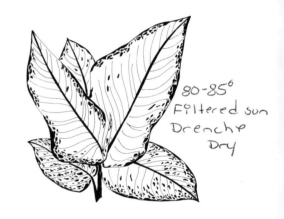

Propagated by stem section cuttings and air layering.

13. Monstera (Swiss cheese plant)
M. deliciosa
mon STER a   de li ci O sa
Southern Mexico.
A vining plant having *large*, leathery, deeply cut or perforated leaves and *aerial roots*. The juvenile form is known as *Philodendron pertusum*. *Deliciosa* probably refers to the edible fruit. Leaves are up to 3 feet long. Only mature plants have holes in the leaves. Does best in partial shade.

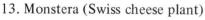

Propagated by leaf bud cuttings.

80-85°
Filtered sun
moist

14. Nephthytis
Syngonium podophyllum
syn GO ni um   po do PHYLL um
Mexico to Costa Rica.
Foliage plant with *arrowhead* or shield-shaped leaves with long petioles—often used in planters. *Podophyllum* means "foot and leaf," probably in allusion to the stout petioles. Does best in partial shade. Seedlings have basal leaves, but become vine-like with age.

Commercially propagated by seeds. Propagated by stem tip cuttings or by dividing the rhizomes.

15. Philodendron
P. ~~oxycardium~~ scandens
phil o DEN dron   ox y CAR di um
Brazil.
A trailing plant with heart-shaped leaves. Tolerates part sun to shade. Soil should be allowed to dry out slightly before being watered again. There are many other species of philodendrons commonly used as houseplants.

Propagated by stem tip cuttings as well as leaf bud cuttings.

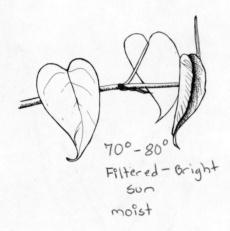

70°-80°
Filtered – Bright
sun
moist

16. Pothos (devil's ivy)
~~*Scindapsus aureus*~~ Epipremnum aureum
scin DAP sus   AU re us
Solomon Islands.
Climbing or trailing foliage plant with waxy, dark green leaves with *yellow* variegation. (*Aureus* refers to golden.) Many other horticultural varieties are available with cream or white markings. Leaves increase in size with maturity. Becomes rampant. It should be allowed to dry out considerably between waterings. Does best in a well-lighted place, but not in direct sun. In a shady place the leaf markings will gradually disappear.

Propagation is similar to that of philodendron.

80-85°
Filtered sun
moist or Drench & Dry

Family: Araliaceae
a ra li A ce ae
Aralia or Ginseng Family
Mostly woody plants having alternate leaves and grown for their foliage.
Number of Genera: 105   Species: 1,400

17. English Ivy
Hedera helix genus Too
HED er a   HE lix
Europe, Asia, North Africa.
A trailing plant with many varieties. Leaves are five-lobed and glossy green when young. This is a woody vine that is evergreen and hardy. Requires cool temperatures (50° to 65°F). Can be grown indoors in winter in bowls of water. This is the ivy of "The Holly and the Ivy" and was used by colonists on mantels at Christmastime. Green glass bowls are excellent for displaying vines during the Christmas season.

Propagated by stem tip cuttings.

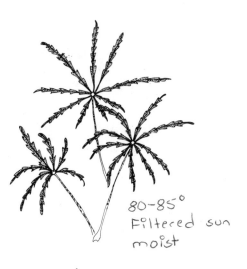

5-lobed
55-60° DT
house
Bright light
moist

18. False Aralia
Dizygotheca elegantissima
di zy go THE ca   el e gan TISS i ma
New Hebrides.
Showy plant having *palmately compound* leaves. The 7 to 11 leaflets are long and very slender. Does best in warm air with high humidity and partial shade. The soil needs to be kept on the moist side. The transfer from a greenhouse to a warm, dry room usually results in considerable leaf drop unless the plants have been properly conditioned.

Propagation by stem or root cuttings.

80-85°
Filtered sun
moist

19. Fatshedera (tree ivy)
X *F. lizei*
fats HED er a   LI ze i
A *bigeneric hybrid* between *Fatsia japonica* and *Hedera helix* (Fatshedera). Found as a chance seedling in France among *Fatsia* seedlings and introduced to the U.S. in 1926. Has attractive, *five-lobed*, dark green leaves. Good for planters. Keep the soil moist. Does best in sun or partial sun, and can withstand *low* temperatures down to 25°F. The X before the genus indicates that the genus is a hybrid.

Propagated by stem tip or leaf bud cuttings.

55-60°
Bright sun
moist

20. Umbrella Tree (schefflera)
Brassaia actinophylla
BRASS ai a   ac tin o PHYLL a
Australia, Java.

Has large palmately compound leaves that form rosettes at the end of branches similar to an umbrella. Often used with palms for decorating stages. Will withstand low light intensities, but a light place is more beneficial. Before watering again, be sure the soil is on the dry side.

Propagated by stem tip cuttings and seeds.

Family: Araucariaceae
a rau ca ri A ce ae
Araucaria Family
A family of evergreen trees that are not hardy.
Number of Genera: 2   Species: 32

70°
filtered sun
moist

21. Norfolk Island Pine
Araucaria heterophylla
a rau CA ri a   het er o PHYLL a
Norfolk Island in the South Pacific.
An *evergreen* tree grown as a potted plant in greenhouses and homes. When young, the branches are in tiers and the needles are dark green. Leaves are spirally arranged and stiff. Does best in cool temperatures and partial shade. Don't overwater. Let the top soil at ½-inch depth dry out between waterings.

Only terminal cuttings will develop into well-rounded plants; cuttings from side shoots develop into one-sided plants. Can also be grown from seed.

Family: Asclepiadaceae
as clep i a DA ce ae
Milkweed Family
Herbs, shrubs, and vines with milky juice and regular flowers.
Number of Genera: 220   Species: 2,000

22. String of Hearts (rosary vine)
Ceropegia woodii
cer o PE gi a   WOOD i i
Asia, Africa, Malaya.
A *trailing* plant with small, opposite, fleshy, heart-shaped leaves and purplish flowers. Small bulbs or tubers form at nodes. Don't over-water. A difficult plant to kill if not over-watered. Because of its succulent habit, let it

dry out between waterings. Grow it in a semi-shady to sunny location.

Propagated by stem tip cuttings or by tubers.

23. Wax Plant
Hoya carnosa
HOY a   car NO sa
Queensland, Southern China.
Has very fragrant, waxy, pinkish-white flowers. A climbing *vine* with *thick*, opposite, entire leaves. Let it dry out between waterings. Give it a *sunny* location. There are many varieties with variegated leaves, crinkled leaves, etc.

Propagated by stem tip cuttings.

Family: Balsaminaceae
bal sam i NA ce ae
Balsam Family
Succulent herbs with watery stems, simple leaves, and showy flowers that have spurs.
Number of Genera: 2   Species: 450

24. Impatiens (patient lucy, patience plant, busy
              lizzie)
I. spp.
im PA ti ens
Zanzibar.
Can be grown outdoors in summer as a bedding plant in partial or full shade. Indoors it prefers high humidity. A soft, fleshy, succulent plant. It flowers readily and over a long period of time as is indicated in common names. Dwarf varieties are best suited for houseplants.

Propagated by stem tip cuttings and seeds.

Family: Begoniaceae
be go ni A ce ae
Begonia Family
Mostly succulent herbs, often with lop-sided leaves. Male flowers have two petals, female flowers have three to five petals.
Number of Genera: 5   Species: 810

25. Angel-Wing Begonia
Begonia spp.
be GO ni a
Brazil.

Upright plants having thick stems, lopsided leaves, and pinkish, drooping flowers. Keep slightly on the dry side in winter.

Propagate by stem tip cuttings, leaf petiole cuttings, and leaf section cuttings.

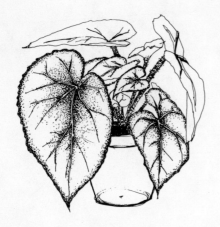

26. Rex Begonia
    B. rex
    be GO ni a   rex
    Assam.
    Has showy, oblique leaves often with interesting patterns. Root is rhizomatous. Prefers shade or bright daylight, but not full sun. Keep slightly on the dry side in winter.

    Propagate by leaf petiole cuttings, leaf section cuttings, and seeds.

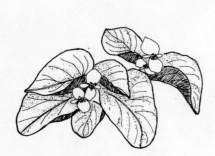

27. Wax Begonia
    B. semperflorens
    be GO ni a   sem per FLOR ens
    Brazil.
    Fibrous-rooted, succulent plants with fleshy, oval leaves. Has many compact branches. *Semperflorens* means everblooming. Grows best indoors in sun. Also excellent as a bedding plant outdoors. Can be kept growing for several years by placing plants outdoors in summer and bringing them back indoors before frost in the fall. They should be cut back and/or divided at this time. To cut back and rejuvenate a plant, remove one-half to two-thirds of the top foliage, trim the remaining tips, shape, and fertilize.

    Propagate by stem tip cuttings and seeds.

Family: Bromeliaceae
        bro me li A ce ae
        Pineapple Family
        Mostly short-stemmed epiphytes with basal leaves in a rosette.
Number of Genera: 50   Species: 2,000

28. Pineapple
    Ananas comosus
    a NA nas   co MO sus
    Tropical America.

Has long leaves in a rosette and bears a dense head at the tip.

Members of this family are referred to as *bromeliads.*

Bromeliads, along with orchids, are the aristocrats of the flowering plant world. All bromeliads are native to the tropical and subtropical regions of the Americas where most are airplants that grow on trees. Not parasites, they derive their food from nutrients found in rainwater and debris. A few species like the pineapple and the beautiful earthstars grow in the soil.

Their shape is usually in the form of a rosette, their foliage is either plain or unusually marked, and all bear unusual flowers. Bromeliads are ideally suited for indoor culture and will thrive in warm, dry, air-conditioned rooms.

80-85°
Bright sun
moist

Care of Bromeliads

Light: Like most other houseplants, bromeliads grow best when given the most light possible. Species differ in their preference for the amount of light, however, so pick your plant to match the location in which it will live. Bromeliads with thin green leaves and smooth edges prefer medium light (e.g., *Vriesia, Neoregelia, Nidularium*). Those with thick leaves with teeth along the edges and whitish markings prefer high light (e.g., *Aechmea, Billbergia*). Those with grass-like leaves and the succulent varieties do best if given full sun for part or all of the day (e.g., *Tillandsia, Dyckia,* pineapple).

Water: The rosette of most bromeliads forms a "cup" that will hold water in the base of the leaves. Tapwater can be used to fill the cup but rainwater is best. Water should be slightly acid (pH 6.0 to 6.5) for best growth. The potting medium should be watered when the surface becomes dry. For added beauty, give them a good bath under the faucet once a week. Bromeliads grown on bark or treefern slabs should be misted with water two or three times per week. *Note*: The white "scaly" surface of the leaves is not to be wiped away; these are

88

cells that act like sponges that absorb moisture from the air.

Fertilizer: Feed bromeliads at monthly intervals with liquid fertilizer at half the strength recommended on the container label. Feed directly into the cup with some solution poured into the soil. Plants on bark or treefern slabs should be misted with the fertilizer solution or dipped in it.

Life Cycle: When the parent plant is mature, it flowers once. Flowers last from a few weeks to 6 months. As the plant matures, offsets develop which will mature and flower in 1 to 2 years. Offsets can be cut off the parent plant when they are about one-third the size of the parent and planted in a porous growing medium such as an equal mixture of peat moss and perlite. Offsets will root in this medium if it is kept evenly moist.

This information was supplied by L. F. Wilson.

Family: Cactaceae
cac TA ce ae
Cactus Family
Succulents with fleshy, thickened stems (usually spiny) and showy flowers.
Number of Genera: 150   Species: 1,800

29. Christmas Cactus
Schlumbergera bridgesii
schlum ber GER a   BRIDGE si i
Brazil.
Flowering plant with flat, leaf-like jointed stems. To flower, it requires long nights or periods of darkness without light (12 hours or more). *Cool temperatures* will also help to insure flowering. Should be placed out-of-doors in the summer, preferably in a cool, shaded location, and watered frequently. Since this is the active growing season, the plants should also be fertilized. This cactus requires a humus-type soil. Bring indoors before frost.

Propagated by stem tip cuttings with two or three branch segments.

30. Opuntia
    O. spp.
    o PUN ti a
    North, Central, and South America.
    There are hundreds of species ranging from small plants to trees. Several species are native to the northern U.S. *O. microdasys* is the bunny-ears shown here; it is used in dish gardens. Most cacti tolerate full sun and make excellent houseplants if not overwatered. During their dormant period in mid-winter, reduce watering. To induce flowering place in cool location (40° to 50°F) during dormancy.

    Commonly propagated by stem section cuttings and by seeds.

70°
Bright sun
Drench &
Dry

Family: Commelinaceae
com me li NA ce ae
Spiderwort Family
Plants mostly with alternate, showy leaves on succulent, watery stems. Flowers usually with three sepals and three petals.
Number of Genera: 37   Species: 600

31. Callisia
    C. elegans
    cal LIS i a   EL e gans
    Southeastern Mexico.
    Vigorous little creeper with triangular, clasping leaves that are green with white stripes. Prefers bright light.

    Propagated by stem tip cuttings. Place several rooted cuttings (three to five) in a 5- or 6-inch pot.

32. Moses in the Cradle (Moses in the bullrushes)
    Rhoeo spathacea
    RHOE o   spath a CE a
    Mexico.
    Leaves lance-shaped and green above, purple below. Above each leaf base, two large boat-like bracts hold little white flowers. Prefers bright light.

    Propagated by stem tip cuttings, offsets, and seeds.

70°
Filtered
sun
moist

33. Purple Heart
Setcreasea ~~purpurea~~ pallida
set CREA se a   pur PUR e a
Mexico.
Has purple, lance-shaped leaves on erect, fleshy stems.

Propagated by stem tip cuttings. Place several cuttings in a 6-inch pot (around the edges) if you want to use it as a hanging basket.

34. Tahitian Bridal Veil
Gibasis geniculata
gi BA sis   ge NIC u la ta
Tropical America.
Small, fine-textured creeper that does well in hanging baskets, producing many small white flowers. Does not become leggy or rampant like many others in the family.

Easily propagated by stem tip cuttings.

35. Tradescantia (giant white inch plant)
T. albiflora 'Albo-vittata'
tra des CAN ti a al bi FLOR a AL bo vit TA ta
Central America.
Has variegated, coarse leaves 2 to 3¼ inches long. Variegation pattern is usually the same all over the plant except for an occasional green shoot. Does best in bright areas out of direct sunlight.

Propagated by stem tip cuttings which can also be rooted in water.

36. Tradescantia
T. fluminensis 'Variegata'
tra des CAN ti a   flu mi NEN sis   var ie GA ta
Argentia, Brazil.
Leaf variegation pattern varies from leaf to leaf (leaves are 1 inch long). Sometimes all green or all creamy-white shoots emerge. Remove all entirely green shoots or else the entire plant will revert to the green form.

Propagated by stem tip cuttings. Take only the variegated shoots since shoots having only creamy-white leaves won't root because of lack of chlorophyll (no photosynthesis).

37. Trailing Callisia
    Callisia repens
    cal LIS i a   RE pens
    A small-leaved, drooping plant that produces many stems that hang straight down. Leaves are about 1 inch long and are green on both sides. Does not usually produce flowers. Stems will droop for 6 or 8 feet until they touch the floor. Broken pieces of stem root easily and run all over the floor of a greenhouse.

    Easily propagated by stem tip cuttings.

38. Wandering Jew
    Zebrina pendula
    ze BRI na   PEN du la
    Mexico.
    Fleshy, trailing plant that roots at every node. Leaves deep green to purple above, dark purple below. Leaves have two silver bands. *Z. purpusii* has olive to purplish-brown leaves which are purple above. Leaves of both species are 2 to 2½ inches long.

    Propagated by stem tip cuttings.

70°
Filtered sun
moist

Family: Compositae
com POS i tae
Composite Family
The largest family of vascular plants. Flowers occur in heads with disk flowers in the center and ray flowers on the outside.
Number of Genera: 950   Species: 20,000

39. Chrysanthemum
    C. morifolium
    chrys AN the mum   mor i FO li um
    East Asia.
    The common chrysanthemum does best in full sun. Hardy varieties are cut back twice, the second time around July 4, to induce branching. Has a shallow root system and should be mulched outdoors. Requires long nights to induce flowering. Chrysanthemums offered by florists as houseplants should be discarded after flowering unless you want to try to grow them outside as a perennial (a few varieties may

prove to be hardy). The flowers of cut mums outlast the leaves. Chrysanthemums have many different flower types, including singles, anemone, pompom, spider, tubular petaled, and incurved petaled.

Easily propagated by stem tip cuttings or by division of the crown.

40. Cineraria
Senecio cruentus
sen E ci o   cru EN tus
South Africa.
Showy, flowering gift plant having many daisy-like flowers purple to white in color. Requires cool temperatures (65°F or less). Needs bright light (not direct sunlight). Requires frequent watering. Plants are discarded after flowering. Aphids like this plant.

Propagated by seed, but most indoor gardeners will find this difficult.

41. German Ivy
Senecio mikanioides
sen E ci o   mi ka ni OI des
South Africa.
Twining plant with glossy, bright green, alternated, lobed leaves. Similar to English ivy but not woody, except perhaps at the base of the stems. Needs plenty of water. Grows in partial shade or partial sun. Excellent for window boxes. The variegated variety has rather thick leaves (*S. macroglossus variegatus*).

Propagated by stem tip cuttings.

42. Velvet Plant
Gynura aurantiaca
gy NUR a   au ran ti A ca
Java.
Plants with green leaves having violet or purple hairs. This species becomes tall and needs to be pinched often to keep it from becoming leggy. Leaves are alternate. Needs full light to get full color. A different species (*G. sarmentosa*) has smaller, lobed leaves; more flowers; a spreading habit; and it doesn't need to be pinched as often.

Propagated by stem tip cuttings.

80-85°
Bright light (sun)
moist

Family: Crassulaceae
crass u LA ce ae
Stonecrop Family
Succulent plants with fleshy leaves and
stems. Leaves often in rosettes.
Number of Genera: 33   Species: 1,300

43. Bryophyllum (maternity plant)
Kalanchoe daigremontiana
kal an CHO e   dai gre mont i A na
Madagascar.
Plantlets are produced from the serrations
along the margins of the leaves (commonly
referred to as *viviparous leaves*—leaves that
produce living young). Does best in full sun or
semi-sun with cool temperatures. Not a good
houseplant, but very popular with children.
Leaves up to at least 7 inches long and 1½
inches wide. Other kalanchoes of interest include *K. tomentosa* (panda plant), which has
white, hairy leaves with brown margins. *K.
pinnata* (air plant) will produce plantlets from
the leaf margins if leaves are placed on moist
soil. *K. beauverdii* is a climbing (up to 3 feet)
plant with narrow, incurved leaves.

70°
Bright sun
Drench & Dry

Commonly propagated by plantlets or stem tip
cuttings. The plantlets produced usually have
roots on them and can be potted immediately
in a growing medium.

44. Echeveria
Echeveria spp.
ech e VER i a
Tropical America, Mexico.
This genus includes many species of succulents,
most of which have leaves in a basal rosette.
Grow in bright light in a porous soil mix kept
on the *dry* side.

Propagated by stem tip and leaf petiole cuttings.

45. Jade Plant
Crassula argentea
CRASS u la   ar GEN te a
Cape Province.
Has branching stems and forms a tree-like
plant. Leaves are glossy jade green, turning

94

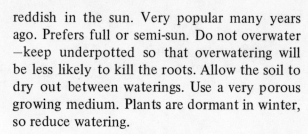

70°
Bright sun
to filtered
Drench' Dry

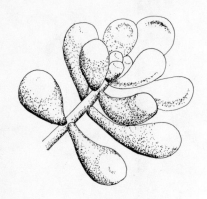

reddish in the sun. Very popular many years ago. Prefers full or semi-sun. Do not overwater —keep underpotted so that overwatering will be less likely to kill the roots. Allow the soil to dry out between waterings. Use a very porous growing medium. Plants are dormant in winter, so reduce watering.

Propagate by stem tip or leaf petiole cuttings.

46. Jelly Beans
Sedum pachyphyllum
SE dum pa chy PHYLL um
Southern Mexico.
Small succulent with fleshy leaves (*Pachyphyllum* means thick-leaved). Prefers full to semi-sun. Don't overwater. Interesting for children. Older leaves tend to fall off if touched, and root easily. Other sedums of interest include *S. morganianum* (burro tail) and the common "hen and chicks," *S. sempervivums*.

Propagate by leaf or stem tip cuttings.

Family: Cyperaceae
cy per A ce ae
Sedge Family
Plants with grass-like leaves or with leaves in terminal umbels. Native mainly to swamps and marshes.
Number of Genera: 72   Species: 3,200

47. Cyperus (umbrella plant)
C. alternifolius
cy PER us al tern i FOL i us
Madagascar.
Upright plant up to 4 feet tall having leaves in terminal umbels. Does best in bright light. This plant cannot be overwatered and should always be kept moist since it is a native of boggy areas. If the plant dries out, the tips of the leaves become brown. Flowers may appear on the umbels. Stems of *C. papyrus* were used by Egyptians as a source of paper.

Propagated by seeds, by divisions, and by placing the base of terminal umbels of leaves in about ½ inch of propagating medium.

70°
Filtered sun
Wet

Family: Euphorbiaceae
eu phor bi A ce ae
Spurge Family
Plants including cactus-like succulents
with alternate leaves, milky sap, and inconspicuous flowers surrounded by colorful bracts.

Number of Genera: 283   Species: 7,300

48. Chenille Plant
Acalypha hispida
a ca LY pha   HIS pi da
India.
Plant with bright green, hairy leaves and long,
bright red flowers in drooping spikes resembling a cat's tail. Does best in sunny to semi-
sunny locations. Becomes tall and leggy, so
pinch repeatedly.

Propagated by stem tip cuttings.

49. Croton
Codiaeum variegatum pictum
co di AE um   var ie GA tum   PIC tum
Ceylon, Malaya, Southern India, Sunda Islands.
Tropical shrubs with colorful, variegated
foliage. Leaves are often twisted. Does best in
sunny to semi-sunny locations. Fresh air circulation is helpful.

Propagated by stem tip cuttings and seeds.

80-85°
Bright sun
moist

50. Crown of Thorns
Euphorbia(splendens) variety milii (species)
eu PHOR bi a   SPLEN dens
Madagascar.
Plant with *small*, short-lived leaves, and stems
covered with stout gray spines. The floral
bracts are ½ to 1 inch across and usually rosy
red. Does best in bright light. Keep on the dry
side, especially in winter. Prefers warm temperatures. Let cuttings dry out several days before
placing in propagating medium. Older plants
require considerable space because of the
freely branching habit of the plant.

Propagated by stem tip cuttings.

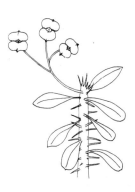

80°
Bright sun
drench & dry

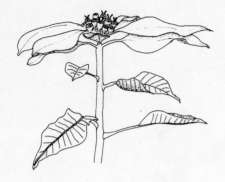

51. Poinsettia
Euphorbia pulcherrima
eu PHOR bi a   pul CHERR i ma
Southern Mexico.
Common Christmas plant with showy bracts. Needs bright light, but not full sunlight. In dark locations, considerable leaf-drop will occur. Does best at a uniform temperature (60° to 70°F, and cooler at night). Keep soil moderately dry. Drafts, dim light, dry air, and improper watering may cause leaves to drop. Very difficult to make it rebloom.

Propagated by stem tip cuttings.

Family: Geraniaceae
ge ra ni A ce ae
Geranium Family
Mostly herbaceous plants with alternate leaves. Often scented. Showy flowers, usually in umbels.
Number of Genera: 11   Species: 850

52. Geranium
Pelargonium hortorum
pel ar GO ni um   hor TOR um
South Africa.
A very popular garden bedding plant. Also widely used in outdoor planters and window boxes. Does best in bright light and cool temperatures (about 55°F at night). Rather slow-growing—requires several months for cuttings or seedlings to develop into good-sized flowering plants. Keep soil on the dry side, not constantly moist.

Propagated by stem tip cuttings. Some newer varieties are propagated by seeds.

Family: Gesneriaceae
ges ner i A ce ae
Gesneria Family
Tropical plants with opposite or basal leaves and showy flowers.
Number of Genera: 85   Species: 1,200

53. African Violet
Saintpaulia ionantha
saint PAUL i a   i o NAN tha
Coastal region of East Africa.

The basal leaves have long petioles. Grown for its showy flowers. Prefers warm temperatures. Cold water on the leaves will spot them. Will tolerate sun in the winter, but not in the summer. Does well under fluorescent lights and is often grown in basements using them.

Commonly propagated by leaf petiole cuttings and by dividing the crown.

54. Episcia (flame violet)
    E. cupreata
    e PIS ci a   cu pre A ta
    Columbia.
    A tropical creeper with handsome foliage and showy flowers. Useful in hanging baskets. Prefers shade, but will stand some sun.

    Commonly propagated by stem tip cuttings and also by leaf petiole cuttings.

55. Gloxinia
    Sinningia speciosa
    sin NIN gi a   spe ci O sa
    Brazil.
    A rather common, handsome flowering plant often sold as a gift plant in spring. Prefers warm temperatures. Does well under fluorescent lights. Can stand some sun. Let soil gradually dry out after plant has flowered. Remove dried dead leaves. Tubers can be stored in a basement during their rest period in autumn and can be repotted at the beginning of the year. Plant tuber at soil level in a porous medium of about ½ soil and ½ peat. Increase watering as leaves appear. Keep fully grown plant moist all the time, but not waterlogged. This is the main cause of the failure of buds to develop, so-called bud-blasting. Gloxinias have velvety-looking flowers that are available in a variety of colors. Double-flowering plants are also available.

    Commonly propagated by seeds, leaf petiole cuttings, and stem cuttings.

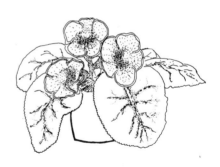

56. Streptocarpus
    S. saxorum
    strept o CAR pus   sax OR um
    Africa.

Bushy plant with many fleshy, oval leaves. Has delicate, lavender-blue flowers on long, thin stems. Culture is similar to episcia.

Propagated by stem tip cuttings.

Family: Labiatae
la bi A tae
Mint Family
Plants have square stems, opposite leaves, and irregular flowers. Leaves and sap are usually aromatic.

Number of Genera: 200   Species: 3,200

57. Coleus
C. ~~blumei~~ xhybridus
CO le us   BLU me i
Java.
Erect plant, usually with colorful *foliage*. Needs to be *pinched* often. Does best in partial to full sun. A very popular plant for indoors and out. Fancy-leaved types are offered in spring as bedding plants. The 'Trailing Queen' varieties make very showy hanging baskets and need not be pinched.

Commonly propagated by stem tip cuttings and by seeds.

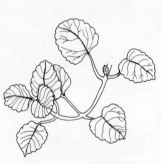

58. Plectranthus (Swedish ivy)
P. spp.
plec TRAN thus
Australia, Pacific Islands.
P. australis is a creeping plant suitable for hanging baskets. The waxy green leaves are almost *round*. Does best in filtered sunlight. *P. coleoides* 'Marginatus' is similar to *P. australis*, but with smaller leaves (up to 2 inches long) having crenate leaf margins which are white. Leaves are very aromatic.

Commonly propagated by stem tip cuttings.

Family: Leguminosae
le gu mi NO sae
Pea Family
Plants usually with pinnately compound leaves.

Number of Genera: 550   Species: 13,000

59. Sensitive Plant
Mimosa pudica
mi MO sa   PU di ca
Brazil.
Plant with bipinnate, sensitive leaves and long petioles. Commonly grown as a houseplant, but sometimes placed outdoors in summer. Leaflets respond best to heat (such as a match placed beneath the tips), to touch (pencil or finger), to wind (blow on the leaves), and to jarring. The more severe the stimulus, the quicker and greater will be the response. Responses are caused by changes in *turgor pressure* (normal turgidity) in certain cells.

Rather easily grown from seeds, which can be ordered through many different companies.

80-85°
Filtered sun
moist

Family: Liliaceae

lil i A ce ae
Lily Family
Perennial plants that usually die down after flowering to a bulb or bulb-like organ. Flowers are regular and six-parted.
Number of Genera: 175   Species: 2,000

60. Aloe
A. spp.
a LO e
South Africa.
Succulent plants that form a rosette of leaves. Prefer partial to full sun. Don't overwater. Several are grown as houseplants. The resin of the leaves of several species is sometimes used for medicinal purposes.

Suckers from the bases of the plant can be used for propagation.

61. Baby Smilax
Asparagus asparagoides myrtifolius
as PAR a gus as par i GOI des myr ti FO li us
South Africa.
Small-leaved climber used in wedding (and other) decorations. Tolerates shade to semi-sun.

Propagated by seeds.

80-85°
Filtered
sun
Drench P
Dry

70°
Filtered
sun
moist

80-85°
Filtered sun
Wet

62. Birdsnest Sansevieria   Agavaceae family
Sansevieria trifasciata 'Hahnii'
san se VIER i a tri fas ci A ta HAH ni i
New Orleans.
This plant was patented in 1953. It is a low plant having leaves in a *rosette*. Sun or shade.

Commonly propagated by division or by leaf section cuttings.

63. Cast-Iron Plant
Aspidistra elatior
as pi DIS tra e LA ti or
China.
Large, tough, leathery, blackish-green foliage. Shade to semi-sun. Can withstand low temperatures. Old-fashioned parlor plant. A more attractive variegated form is sometimes offered.

Propagate by dividing the roots.

64. Chlorophytum (spider plant, airplane plant)
C. comosum 'Vittatum'
chlor o PHY tum co MO sum vit TA tum
Africa.
Plant having white-edged, linear leaves in a rosette. Long racemes of small flowers are borne on runners (or stolens) under short days (long nights) and develop into new plants after flowering.

Commonly propagated by seeds and by removing the aerial plants.

65. Dracena (corn plant)   Agavaceae
Dracaena fragrans
dra CAE na FRA grans
Guinea, Ethiopia.
Handsome foliage plant with large, long, green, leathery, sessile leaves having parallel veins. All dracenas should be kept moist but not soggy. They can be grown under artificial light or filtered light, but not in full sun.

Propagated by stem tip cuttings.

66. Dracena   Agavaceae
Dracaena ~~marginata~~ cincta or concinna
dra CAE na mar gi NA ta
Madagascar.

Has linear, dark green leaves with narrow, red margins. Older plants have trunk-like stems with terminal rosettes because the oldest leaves drop off. Plants can withstand low light intensities and low humidity.

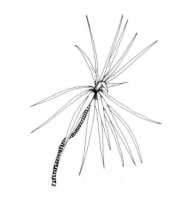

Propagated by stem tip cuttings and stem section cuttings.

67. Dracena   Agavaceae
Dracaena sanderiana
dra CAE na   san der i A na
Cameroons, Congo.
Most common of the dracenas, it has deep green leaves and long petioles. Leaves have white bands and are 5 to 9 inches long. Keep the soil moist. Other dracenas which are frequently used include *D. deremensis*, with white-striped leaves, and *D. godseffiana*, with broad, yellow-spotted leaves.

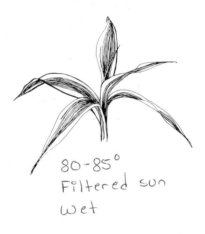

80-85°
Filtered sun
wet

Propagated by stem tip cuttings. All dracenas can also be propagated by stem section cuttings. Place a stem section of 1 to 2 inches in a pot and cover the stem with the propagating medium. Place the pot (after watering) in a plastic bag. Have patience because it can take a long time for young plants to appear.

68. Easter Lily
Lilium longiflorum 'Croft'
LIL i um   long i FLOR um
Japan.
This variety was developed in the Pacific Northwest. Keep in a cool, draft-free location having strong light in order to prolong the blooming period. Usually discarded after flowering, but may be planted outdoors in late May after the foliage dries up. Not reliably hardy.

69. Hyacinth
Hyacinthus orientalis
hy a CIN thus   or i en TAL is
Greece to Asia Minor and Syria.
Bulbous plant commonly used for forcing. Flowers are very fragrant. Bulbs are relatively hardy. After flowering, let the foliage grow until it starts to yellow. Then gradually withhold water until the tops dry up. The bulbs can

then be stored until late summer when they can be planted outdoors in the garden or in flower beds. The size of the flower spikes will decrease, but there will be more spikes having fewer flowers.

Hyacinths can also be grown in water in "hyacinth glasses," now often made of plastic. Place the bulb on the container and fill the container with water to the base of the bulb. Place the hyacinth in a dark closet or basement, checking the water level regularly and adding water as needed. Hyacinths are ready to be brought out into your home when the sprouts are 2 inches long or when the flower spikes can be seen or felt. If hyacinths are brought into the living room too early, the flower spikes won't elongate. If this occurs, placing hyacinths back in darkness will usually help. Expose hyacinths gradually to high light and to warm temperatures. Hyacinths forced by this method should be discarded after flowering since it is difficult to transplant the rooted bulb in the soil outdoors.

Propagated by bulbs.

70. Snake Plant (mother-in-law tongue)
Sansevieria trifasciata   Agavaceae
san se VIER i a   tri fas ci A ta
Tropical Africa, India.
Common houseplant with erect, leathery leaves up to 4 feet long. Does well in sun or shade. The variegated form cannot be maintained by leaf section cuttings. For best results, let plants become slightly pot-bound. Leaves of snake plant can be used in flower arrangements to add vertical lines. If the leaves are in water for a long time, they might form roots. Two different upright snake plants are commonly grown. *S. trifasciata* has green leaves with dark, irregular bands across the leaves. *S. t. laurentii* has similar leaves, but they have margins which are creamy white. This variegated plant is a *chimera* (a mixture of tissues of different genetic constitution in the same part of a plant), with the genetic make-up of the leaf margins being different from that in the center of the leaf. Since new plants produced by leaf

80-85°
Filtered sun
moist or Drench & Dry

section cuttings usually develop from the center of the leaf, they will show the features of *S. trifasciata*.

Propagated by leaf section cuttings or by divisions.

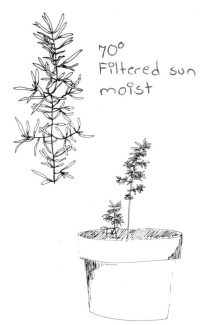

70°
Filtered sun
moist

71. Sprenger Asparagus
    Asparagus densiflorus 'Sprengeri'
    as PAR a gus den si FLOR us SPREN ger i
    South Africa.
    Has needle-like leaves about 1 inch long on thorny stems. Good for hanging baskets. Does best in shade to semi-sun. *A. plumosus* (asparagus fern) is a very fine-textured species commonly used in flower arrangements. *A. d.* 'Meyers' is a very desirable new variety that gives a very fluffy appearance.

    Propagated by seeds or by dividing clumps.

72. Ti Plant (pronounced as tea) Agavaceae
    Cordyline terminalis 'Ti'
    cor dy LI ne   ter mi NAL is
    Eastern Asia.
    Leaves are usually crowded at the end of the stem and have distinct, narrowed, channeled petioles. Has broad (3 inches), shiny, brightly colored leaves about 9 inches long. Leaves are reddish, especially the youngest leaves. Older leaves turn dark brown or dark red. Leaves are sometimes used in flower arrangements. Occasionally, ads appear in magazines offering cane sections from Hawaii or other states. Does best in semi-sun to shade.

    Commonly propagated by stem tip cuttings. Information presented earlier on stem section cuttings of dracenas and dumbcanes also applies to these plants.

73. Tulip
    Tulipa spp.
    tu LI pa
    Mediterranean region, Asia, Japan.
    Very common, hardy plants with showy flowers grown from bulbs. Often used for forcing. *Tulipa* is from an oriental word for turban. Keep in a cool location, especially at night, to prolong the flowering period. Water

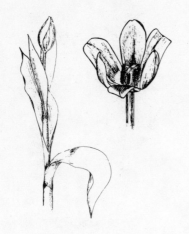

generously. After foliage starts to turn yellow, gradually withhold water until the leaves dry up. Bulbs can be planted outdoors in the fall.

When buying tulips as cut flowers, be sure to get them when the flowers are still in the bud stage. To extend the life of cut flowers, move them to a cooler room at night.

About 800 varieties of tulips are grown commercially. A few varieties have been in cultivation for about 300 years and are the survivors of the "Tulipomania"—a time when huge amounts of money were offered for a single bulb.

Propagated by bulbs.

Family: Malvaceae
mal VA ce ae
Mallow Family
Plants having alternate, palmately veined leaves and showy flowers.
Number of Genera: 50   Species: 1,000

74. Flowering Maple
Abutilon spp.
a BU ti lon
Brazil.
Showy plants having drooping branches with variegated leaves that are about 2 inches long. Flowers are also showy. Leaves are mottled (green and ivory-white speckled) and have stipules. Does best in sunny locations. Several hybrids are available commercially.

Propagated by stem tip cuttings.

Family: Marantaceae
ma ran TA ce ae
Arrowroot Family
Plants with handsome leaves having a feathered pattern design.
Number of Genera: 26   Species: 350

75. Prayer Plant
Maranta leuconeura kerchoveana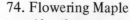
ma RAN ta leu co NEU ra ker cho ve A na
Brazil.
Plant up to 1 foot tall having brown-to-green

80 – 85° DT
filtered sun
moist

blotches on either side of the midribs in the leaves. Leaves fold upward in the evening. Prefers semi-shade. Keep on the dry side during the winter. *M. l. massangeana* is another interesting species, with red, protruding veins and dark brown patches between them.

Propagated by stem tip cuttings.

Family: Moraceae
mo RA ce ae
Mulberry Family
Vines, shrubs, and trees grown for edible fruit or handsome foliage.
Number of Genera: 73   Species: 1,000

76. Creeping Fig
Ficus pumila
FI cus PU mi la
Australia, China, Japan.
Creeping plant with small, heart-shaped leaves when young. Cannot be allowed to dry out. It will climb if given a chance.

Propagated by stem tip cuttings.

77. Fiddle-Leaf Fig
Ficus lyrata
FI cus ly RA ta
Tropical West Africa.
Has fiddle-shaped leaves over a foot long. A very handsome plant. Commonly used in offices, entrance ways, and places where large plants are needed. Many individuals tend to overwater their fig plants, and this results in the formation of brown spots near the edges of the leaves. Occasionally attacked by scale, probably more so than the rubber plant. Wash foliage off occasionally.

Propagated by air layering or by stem cuttings.

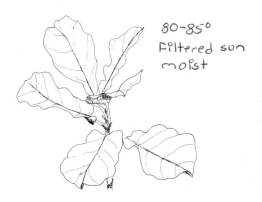

80-85°
Filtered sun
moist

78. Rubber Plant
Ficus elastica
FI cus e LAS ti ca
India, Malaya.
One of the most common houseplants. Has leathery, dark green leaves several inches long. Wash foliage off occasionally with a wet sponge. *Ficus* will tolerate semi-sun to shade.

80-85°
Filtered sun
moist

The first rubber was used for making erasers and was obtained by making cuts in the bark of *Ficus* trees. There are several variegated cultivars. Newly purchased rubber plants should be hardened off or else they may drop some of their lower leaves while becoming acclimated to dry living rooms.

Propagate by air layering or by leaf bud cuttings.

Family: Onagraceae
o na GRA ce ae
Evening-Primrose Family
Herbs and shrubs with usually four-part, showy flowers.
Number of Genera: 20   Species: 650

79. Fuchsia
F. X *hybrida*
FUCH sia
Mexico, South America.
Leaves are simple, ovate (1½ to 4 inches long), and toothed. Plants flower indoors from March to November and longer. They prefer a *cool*, humid atmosphere with partial sun. Whiteflies and mites may be a serious problem indoors. Many horticultural varieties (mostly hybrids) are offered. Fuchsias are not recommended as houseplants unless a cool place can be provided. If you bring them indoors from the garden before frost, prune the plants back considerably.

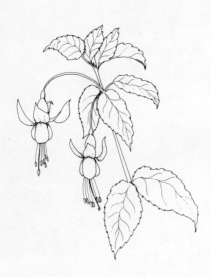

Propagated by stem tip cuttings.

Family: Orchidaceae
or chi DA ce ae
Orchid Family
Epiphytic and terrestrial plants having very showy, irregular flowers.
Number of Genera: 450   Species: 10,000 to 15,000

80. Orchid
Cattleya spp.
catt LEY a
This is the common orchid sold by florists for corsages (usually at Easter). It is large and showy, is an epiphyte, and should be grown in

osmunda (fern roots) or shredded bark. Requires shading and high humidity. Through hybridization, thousands of new varieties are being developed.

Commonly propagated by division.

81. Orchid
Cymbidium spp.
cym BI di um
A terrestrial orchid having smaller flowers than the *Cattleya*, but usually many flowers are produced on a stem. Flowers are often used in corsages during the winter months, and last many weeks. Does best with cool temperatures, rich soil, and light shade.

Commonly propagated by division.

Family: Palmaceae
pal MA ce ae
Palm Family
Chiefly tropical plants having large, leathery, ornamental leaves, fan-shaped or feathery, with parallel veins.
Number of Genera: 210   Species: 4,000

82. Parlor Palm
Chamaedorea elegans
cham ae DO re a   EL e gans
Mexico.
Small, graceful palm eventually becoming 6 to 8 feet tall. Pinnate leaves are loosely spirally arranged.

Propagated best by suckers and commercially by seeds.

80-85° DT
No direct sun
moist

Family: Piperaceae
pi pe RA ce ae
Pepper Family
Plants with insignificant flowers. Leaves have smooth edges and are often succulent.
Number of Genera: 12   Species: 600

83. Emerald Ripple Peperomia
P. caperata
pep er O mi a   ca per A ta
Brazil.

80-85°
Filtered sun
Drench & dry

70°
Filtered
Drench & Dry

A popular peperomia having corrugated leaves and slender flower stalks. Most peperomias make excellent houseplants if not overwatered. They grow best in partial sun or shade, should be allowed to dry out between waterings, and should never be kept on the moist side. The root system is small and shallow.

Usually propagated by leaf petiole cuttings.

84. Peperomia
P. obtusifolia
pep er O mi a   ob tu si FO li a
Venezuela.
Probably the most popular peperomia, growing to about a foot tall. Leaves are obovate or spatulate and 2 to 3 inches long, pale green beneath. Several varieties having silver or gold variegated leaves are available.

Commonly propagated by stem tip cuttings. Can also be propagated by leaf bud cuttings and leaf petiole cuttings.

85. Peperomia
P. rubella
pep er O mi a   ru BELL a
Mexico.
An upright, branching plant with small whorled leaves and hairy stems. Leaves are red beneath. Good for terrariums.

Propagated by stem tip cuttings.

86. Pepper
Piper ornatum
PI per   or NA tum
Celebes.
Very attractive climbing plant grown for its handsome foliage. Leaves are 3 to 4 inches long, green with silver-pink markings. Does best in filtered sun with the soil kept rather moist. It is sometimes confused with philodendron, but philodendron has heart-shaped leaves. Pepper also has a distinct venation pattern. The undersides of pepper leaves have small crystallized droplets or exudates on them resembling insect eggs.

Propagated by stem tip cuttings.

87. Watermelon Peperomia
   P. sandersii argyreia
   pep er O mi a   san DER si i
   Brazil.
   A popular plant having silver markings in the attractive leaves. It is easy to overwater this species.

   Commonly propagated by leaf petiole cuttings, which take many weeks to root and many more weeks to form a new plant.

80-85°
Filtered sun
Drench &
Dry

Family: Pittosporaceae
   pit to spo RA ce ae
   Pittosporum Family
   Plants with thick, alternate (seemingly whorled), leathery leaves. Mainly from Australia.
Number of Genera: 9   Species: 200

88. Pittosporum
   P. tobira
   pit to SPOR um   to BI ra
   China, Japan.
   Woody plant that tends to grow in flat planes. The leaves appear to be whorled. It can be pruned and is used in bonsai. Does best in partial sun with cool temperatures. Misting the foliage is beneficial. A variegated form is available.

   Propagated by stem tip cuttings.

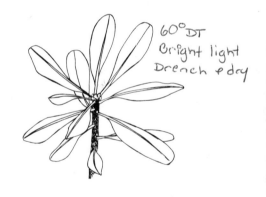

60° DT
Bright light
Drench & dry

Family: Podocarpaceae
   po do car PA ce ae
   Podocarpus Family
   Evergreen trees and shrubs.
Number of Genera: 7   Species: 100

89. Podocarpus
   P. macrophyllus
   po do CAR pus   mac ro PHYLL us
   Japan.
   A coniferous evergreen tree grown in pots as a houseplant. These non-hardy plants have slender, leathery leaves spirally arranged, about 2 to 4 inches long. Does best in semi-shade in cool temperatures. A good and easily grown houseplant if not overwatered.

   Propagated by stem tip cuttings or seeds.

110

Family: Polypodiaceae
pol y po di A ce ae
Fern Family
The largest family of ferns.

Number of Genera: 170   Species: 7,000

90. Boston Fern
Nephrolepis exaltata bostoniensis
ne PHROL e pis ex al TA ta bos to ni EN sis
Florida to Brazil, Africa, South Asia, Australia.
Probably the most common fern grown in homes. Can grow in rather dark places. Double-potting is recommended to provide high humidity. Placing sphagnum moss on top of the soil could also provide high humidity if it is kept wet. Placing the pot on a larger saucer or tray covered with wet gravel would also be beneficial. Many cultivars are available.

Propagated by division, rhizomes, and spores (if produced).

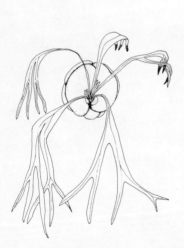

♂ 70°
Filtered
sun
moist

91. Staghorn Fern
Platycerium bifurcatum
plat y CER i um   bi fur CA tum
Australia, New Guinea, New Caledonia.
A coarse-textured fern with forked fronds. Can be grown on osmunda fern roots in pots or on slabs of wood. Immerse the root system in a pail of lukewarm water for about 10 minutes once or twice a week, depending on the humidity and temperature of the room. Allow excess water to drain before placing the plant back. Brown areas may appear on the undersides of mature leaves at the tips. These are the sporangia, which produce spores and which are normal and not harmful. Do not wipe off the grayish layer on the surface of the leaves. If the leaves are attacked by scale, remove the insects by hand and wash the leaves off. Ferns are very susceptible to damage from the use of insecticides.

Propagated by suckers and spores.

70°
No direct sun
moist

92. Table Fern
Pteris ensiformis
PTER is   en si FORM is
Himalayas to Ceylon, Queensland, Samoa.

Another very popular fern. Young plants are often used in terrariums.

Propagated by spores.

Family: Primulaceae
prim u LA ce ae
Primula Family
Herbaceous plants having basal leaves and very showy flowers.

Number of Genera: 28   Species: 800

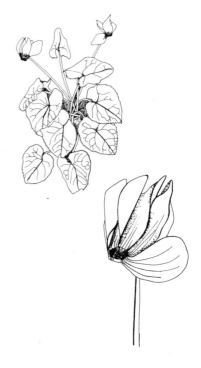

93. Cyclamen
C. persicum
CYC la men   PER si cum.
A tuberous plant having very showy flowers on scapes. A florist's plant sold in winter. Requires good light (but not direct sunlight) and *cool* temperatures (50°F at night and 60° to 65°F during the day). Also requires plenty of water and good drainage. Keep water off the crown. This plant wilts easily, but comes back after watering—use lukewarm water. Remove old flowers by pulling and twisting the flower stem.

Propagated by seeds: it takes about 18 months to produce a flowering plant.

Family: Rutaceae
ru TA ce ae
Rue Family
Perennial herbs to woody plants. Many species are aromatic.

Number of Genera: 100   Species: 1,000

94. Citrus
Citrus spp.
China, Vietnam, Philippines.
Many species make good container plants because of their dark, glossy green leaves. When grown from seeds, the seedlings will not produce the high-quality fruit of the parent. Seedling trees are discarded before they get to be too large and new seedlings are started.

Easily propagated from seeds if they are not allowed to dry out after being removed from the fruit. Soaking the seeds may help.

70°
Bright
light
Drench &
dry

Family: Saxifragaceae
sax i fra GA ce ae
Saxifrage Family
Closely related to the Rose Family and
includes herbs, shrubs, and trees.
Number of Genera: 80   Species: 1,200

95. Pick-a-Back Plant (piggyback)
Tolmiea menziesii
tol MIE a   men ZIE si i
California coast to Alaska.
An interesting plant with light green leaves
which form a rosette. Does best in bright light.
If leaves become mottled, add iron or trace
elements.

Propagated by leaf petiole cuttings with or
without "piggies." Insert the leaf petiole into
the rooting medium so that the base of the
blade is in contact with the medium. Placing a
little of the medium on top of the blade will
help hold the base down on the medium. New
plants develop at the base of the blades.

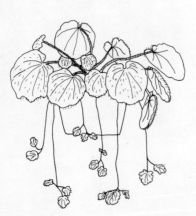

96. Strawberry Begonia (strawberry geranium)
Saxifraga sarmentosa
sax i FRA ga   sar men TO sa
China, Japan.
Small plant with runners. Leaves are rounded
and are arranged in a loose rosette. *Sarmentosa*
means bearing runners. Does best in shade or
partial shade with high humidity. A variegated
form is also available, but it is not as vigorous.

Propagated by runners before or after they
root.

55-60°
Bright sun
Drench & Dry

Family: Scrophulariaceae
scroph u lar i A ce ae
Figwort Family
Plants having opposite leaves and grown
mainly for the showy, irregular flowers.
Square stems.
Number of Genera: 210   Species: 3,000

97. Kenilworth Ivy
Cymbalaria muralis
cym ba LA ri a   mu RAL is
Germany, France, Switzerland.

A small, creeping perennial with rounded leaves and flowers like small snapdragons. Does best in partial sun. Should not be overwatered.

Propagated by stem tip cuttings and from seed. Put several cuttings in a pot for a better display.

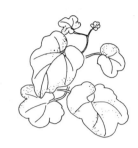

Family: Urticaceae
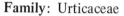
ur ti CA ce ae
Nettle Family
Creeping herbs, shrubs, and trees with simple leaves grown for their foliage.

Number of Genera: 42   Species: 600

98. Aluminum Plant
    Pilea cadierei
    PI le a   ca DIER e i
    Vietnam.
    Introduced recently (in 1952). Upright, branched foliage plants with silver marks in the leaves. Leaves are opposite, about 3 inches long. A dwarf form (*P. c.* 'Minima') is available and is recommended for growing because it doesn't have to be pinched as often.

Propagated by stem tip cuttings.

80-85°
Filtered sun
moist

99. Artillery Plant
    Pilea microphylla
    PI le a   mi cro PHYLL a
    West Indies.
    Small, trailing, much-branched plant with tiny leaves (*microphylls*). Does best in bright light. Artillery plant is so named because of the way pollen is forcibly ejected from the flower. *P. serpillacea* is an *upright form* and is elm-shaped.

Propagated by stem tip cuttings, division, and seeds.

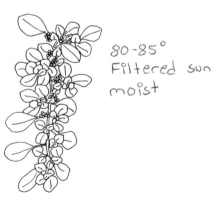

80-85°
Filtered sun
moist

100. Baby's Tears
     Helxine soleiroli
     hel XI ne   so LEIR o li
     Corsica, Sardinia.
     Low, moss-like, creeping foliage plant with tiny leaves. Does best in high humidity, as in a terrarium or a shallow container with the

70°
Filtered sun
moist

114

80-85°
Filtered sun
moist

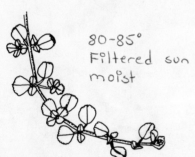

80-85°
Filtered sun
moist

bottom placed in water. A *north* or *east* window would be best. Produces tiny, inconspicuous flowers.

Propagated by dividing small pieces of the mat and transplanting them with roots.

101. Pellionia
P. spp.
pel li O ni a
Vietnam.
A hanging plant with oval leaves. Leaves are greenish-gray in color, netted with black or brown veins. Place three cuttings in a 4-inch pot for a better display.

Propagated by stem tip cuttings.

102. Pilea
P. depressa
PI le a   de PRESS a
Puerto Rico.
Small-leaved, trailing plant with light green leaves. Has inconspicuous white flowers.

Propagated by stem tip cuttings. Place several rooted cuttings in a single pot for better display.

Family: Vitaceae
vi TA ce ae
Grape Family
Mostly woody vines climbing by branched tendrils. Alternate leaves.
Number of Genera: 11   Species: 600

103. Arabian Wax Cissus
Cissus rotundifolia
CIS sus   ro tun di FO li a
East Africa.
Has *rounded*, fleshy leaves and is useful in dish gardens (when young) or as a climbing plant. Older plants produce exudates (secretions) which detract from their appearance, especially when the exudates turn dark because of sooty mold.

Propagated by stem tip cuttings.

104. Grape Ivy
Cissus rhombifolia
CIS sus   rhom bi FO li a
West Indies, North and South America.
Leaves are *three-part*, have brown veins, and are hairy beneath. Not as coarse textured as kangaroo vine. Excellent vine for hanging pots, where the freely hanging branches can be admired. Let soil dry out between waterings.

Propagated by stem tip cuttings. A rooting hormone is beneficial.

105. Kangaroo Vine
Cissus antarctica
CIS sus   ant ARC ti ca
Australia.
Leaves are toothed, dark green, and leathery with brown veins.

Propagated by stem tip cuttings. Cuttings are hard or slow to root without a rooting hormone.

80-85° DT
Filtered sun
moist

70°
Filtered
moist or Drench & Dry

Oxalis
55-60°
Bright sun
Drench & Dry

About watering

Many individuals cannot grow houseplants successfully. This is mainly due to the fact that they overwater their plants. This section on watering may help you obtain a reputation for having a "green thumb" instead of a "brown thumb."

This portion of the book is a program to be read on your own when you feel like learning about watering plants. To use, take a sheet of paper or index card and cover up the responses. Then read the pieces of numbered information (frames) in sequence and uncover the answer(s) in the right-hand column. If you answer the frame correctly, go on to the next one.

This program functions as a teacher. In a sense, we are having a planned conversation, with you responding to questions or information presented. If I do a good job with my part of the conversation, you should learn about watering houseplants.

REASONS FOR WATERING HOUSEPLANTS CORRECTLY

1. Watering houseplants correctly results in plants that live longer, grow faster, and look better.

   If you want to grow attractive, healthy houseplants, you must be able to tell *when* to water plants and also know *how* to water plants.

   People who are known as having "green thumbs," know
   _____ and _____ to water plants.   *when, how*

FACTORS INFLUENCING THE WATERING OF PLANTS

Type of Container

2. There are many factors which determine or influence the watering of plants.

   Familiarity with these _____ will help you deter-   *factors*
   mine _____ and _____ to water plants.   *when, how*

3. One important factor influencing watering is the kind of container or pot in which plants are grown.

   Specifically, you must be aware of the porosity of the
   _____.   *container/pot*

4. Clay pots are porous. Plastic, glass, and metal containers are not porous. Therefore, soil in a clay container will lose _____water vapor than soil in a less porous container.   *more*

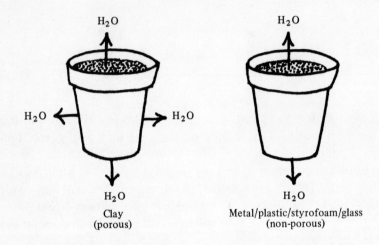

H₂O

H₂O ← → H₂O

H₂O

Clay
(porous)

H₂O

Metal/plastic/styrofoam/glass
(non-porous)

5. Styrofoam and glazed pots are more similar to plastic pots than clay pots as far as porosity is concerned.

   Therefore, styrofoam pots and glazed pots would be _____ porous than clay pots, but_____   *less, more*
   porous than plastic or glass pots.

6. The amount of water and water vapor lost through a pot is important because it affects the frequency of watering.

   Thus, a plant grown in a plastic pot would need to be watered less often than a similar one grown in a _____   *clay/porous*
   container.

7. Many other types of materials are used as containers for growing plants. When using them, you should attempt to estimate what their_____will be so that you will   *porosity*
   have a better idea as to how_____you should   *often/fre-*
   water the plant.   *quently*

8. The regular or common clay flowerpot is still by far the most common container used in growing potted plants. Individuals are *experienced* in growing plants in clay pots because they have been doing it for years.

It should also be pointed out that the porosity of the container not only influences the rate of drying out of growing media, but also influences aeration of media. Root growth is usually better in porous pots.

Chances are that if plants are overwatered in a clay pot, the soil will dry out fairly quickly because the pot is very _____.

porous

9. Likewise, growers know that clay pots (especially brand new ones) should be soaked for a day or two so that the pots will not draw _____ from the soil and dry it out. Young seedlings or transplants are very susceptible to drying out if the clay pots in which they are placed are not _____ before being used.

moisture/water

soaked

10. Because most individuals have a tendency to overwater plants, switching from clay pots to plastic or other non-porous pots can be disastrous if the individual continues to water at the same frequency as he did with the _____ pots. This is because plants grown in non-porous pots _____ _____ to be watered as often as plants grown in _____ pots.

clay

don't need

clay/porous

Size of Plant Relative to Size of Container

11. The size of the plant and the size of the container also influence watering. A small plant in a large pot is said to be *overpotted*.

Similarly, a large plant in a small pot would be called _____.

underpotted

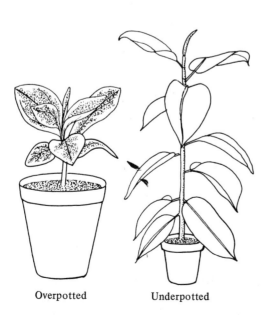

Overpotted   Underpotted

12. Neither overpotting nor underpotting is desirable.

    The underpotted plant needs to be watered _____ *often/frequently*
    because the soil is in constant danger of _____ out. *drying*

13. The overpotted plant has a large amount of soil in relation to
    the shoot and therefore tends to be overwatered. This condi-
    tion often results in the death of the plant because the roots
    _____. *rot*

14. An overpotted plant would probably survive longer in a
    _____ _____ pot than in an impervi- *porous clay*
    ous container made out of _____ , _____ *metal, plastic,*
    or _____ . *styrofoam, etc.*

15. Whether a plant is overpotted or underpotted does not depend
    entirely on the height or width of the plant, but also on the
    size and number of leaves.

    A tall, narrow plant having only a few small leaves could be
    overpotted, whereas a shorter plant in the same size container
    could be potted correctly or even _____ if it had *underpotted*
    either_____small leaves or_____large *many, several*
    leaves.

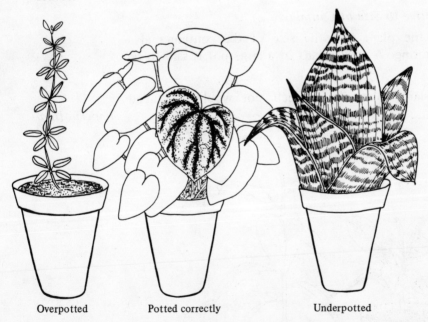

Overpotted   Potted correctly   Underpotted

16. Leaf area, found by multiplying the number of leaves on a
    plant by the size of the leaves, determines the amount of water
    lost by the leaves. Evaporation of water from the leaves of a
    plant is called transpiration.

    Since plants within a species, under similar conditions, transpire
    in proportion to their leaf area, it follows that a plant having

the greater leaf area will transpire or _____ a greater   *lose*   **121**
quantity of_____than a plant having smaller or   *water*
_____ leaves (less leaf area).   *fewer*

Type of Soil

17. The type of soil also affects the watering of plants.

    Soils are commonly classified by the proportion of various
    mineral particles they contain. These particles are defined by
    size, as follows:

Name of Particle	Diameter in Millimeters
Sand	2.00 - 0.02
Silt	0.02 - 0.002
Clay	below 0.002

    A clay soil contains a significant proportion of
    _____particles. Sandy soils consist mostly of   *clay*
    _____particles. Silt particles are more apt to be   *sand*
    present in clay soils than they are in sandy soils. A loam soil is
    a mixture of about half sand and gravel and half silt and clay.
    It is considered to be the best garden soil.

18. Clay soils drain poorly because they lack porosity, but they do
    hold a lot of water.

    Sandy soils are just the opposite of clay; they are very
    _____, but do not hold much _____ .   *porous*
    water/moisture
    Loam soils combine the best properties of clay and sand. They
    are quite _____, but they also hold adequate   *porous*
    _____ .   *water*

19. Clay soils shrink when they dry out. For example, if the soil in
    a pot dries out and forms one hard mass of soil that shrinks
    away from the sides of the pot and rattles if you shake the
    pot, chances are that the soil type is _____ and not   *clay*
    _____.   *sand*

20. If the soil in a pot shrinks very little and doesn't form one
    single hard mass but remains rather loose, the soil is probably
    _____or sandy loam.   *sand*

21. It is not a good idea to use any kind of heavy soil (soil
    containing some clay) for potting up plants. These soils may
    drain well enough in a field where the soil is deep, but not in a
    pot where the soil is _____ .   *shallow*

22. A good demonstration of this can be made using an ordinary sponge. When a thoroughly saturated sponge is held with the shortest side vertical, a certain amount of water will drain out. When it is turned so the longest side is vertical, even more water will drain out.

    Think of the sponge as being full of water columns or tubes. When the tubes are short, gravity does not pull the water away from the surface as much as it does when the tubes are _____ .

    long/deep

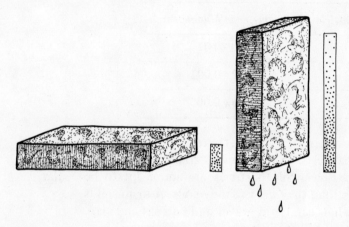

23. A similar situation exists between soil in a pot and soil in a field. After watering a heavy soil in a pot, the soil tends to stay too (wet, dry) around the roots. Therefore, it is much easier to overwater plants in pots than those grown in a garden.

    wet

24. Drainage of soil in a pot can be improved, however, by making tubes or pores larger in diameter. You could do this by adding (coarser, finer) particles to the soil.

    coarser

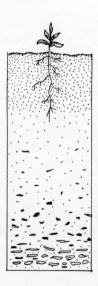

In general, most growing media are probably best described as being mixtures of soil, organic matter, and an inorganic additive.

Peat moss or leaf mold are often used as the _____ _____ Sand and perlite (a heat-treated volcanic material) are common _____ additives which help improve _____ .

organic
matter
inorganic
porosity/drainage

25. Prepackaged or artificial soil mixes are also being used extensively. A mix composed of half peat moss and half vermiculite is very popular. Peat moss is made up of decomposed plants while vermiculite is made from the mineral *mica*. Vermiculite is more porous than peat moss, but not as porous as sand or perlite. This mix is light in weight, moderately porous (if not packed down), and holds a moderate amount of water.

26. It is important to know the type of soil or ingredients in media used for growing plants, because the amount of water that is in the growing medium varies with the _____ of soil.

type

27. Several terms are used in conjunction with the amount of water in soil or growing media.

The amount of water present in the soil after a thorough rain is called the *field capacity*.

You would expect the soil to be _____ at this moisture level.

wet/soggy

28. The amount of water left in the soil at the point when a plant wilts and can't recover is called the *permanent wilting point*.

You would expect the soil to be on the _____ side at this moisture level.

dry

29. The amount of water actually present in soil at the field capacity and the permanent wilting point varies with the type of _____ in the case of field capacity, and with both the type of soil and species of _____ for the _____ _____ _____ .

soil
plant
permanent wilting point

30. For example, two different soil types might contain the following amounts of water at these two levels:

Soil Type	Field Capacity	Permanent Wilting Point
Sandy loam	15%	7%
Clay	30%	16%

124

31. The amount of water in soil between the field capacity and the permanent wilting point is called the *available moisture* and is _____ for use by the plant.

    available

32. According to the chart, the available moisture in a clay soil is much _____ than in a sandy soil because clay soil has a much higher _____ _____, even though the permanent wilting point is also higher.

    greater/higher
    field capacity

33. Although the term "available moisture" refers to the moisture in a soil that a plant can use, it does not follow that roots can absorb the moisture equally well over the entire range. As one might suspect, the moisture in the soil when the soil is near the field capacity is much easier to absorb than moisture in the soil near the _____ _____ _____ .

    permanent
    wilting point

Environmental Factors

34. Environmental factors also influence the frequency of watering by their effect on transpiration rates. Plants transpire at a faster rate when it is warm than when it is cooler. Therefore, you would need to water plants _____ often during warm weather than in cool weather.

    more

35. Similarly, transpiration rates are higher during sunny weather than on dull, overcast days.

    During periods of cloudy or overcast weather conditions, plants would not require watering as often as they would on _____ days.

    sunny

36. From what you have learned, you would expect that plants located in a north window would require _____ frequent watering than plants in a south window.

    less

37. The relative humidity also affects the frequency of watering. Plants transpire at lower rates during humid weather than when the air is _____ .

    dry/less humid

38. *Relative humidity* means the amount of moisture in the air compared with the maximum amount of moisture that the air could hold. The weight of moisture in air is measured in grains (7,000 grains = 1 pound).

    For example, if the relative humidity (R.H.) is 50%, then the air contains only _____ as much moisture as it could hold (100% R.H.).

    half

39. The amount of moisture that air can hold varies with the temperature. Warm air can hold much more moisture than _____ air.

    cold/cool

40. For example, from the following chart you should be able to determine that if air at 20°F and 50% R.H. were heated to 80°F it would then have a relative humidity of about (25%, 6%, 15%).

    6%

Temperature (degrees F)	Relative Humidity (percent)	Amount of Water in 1 lb. of Dry Air (grains)
20	50	10
	100	20
40	50	20
	100	39
60	50	39
	100	78
80	50	78
	100	156

41. The relative humidity of homes is about 30% to 35% at best. Most plants grow better with a much higher humidity than this, but condensation of moisture on windows in winter becomes a problem when the relative humidity is higher than 30% to 35%. In fact, on really cold days, condensation will occur at an even (higher, lower) relative humidity.

    lower

42. Air movement or wind also affects transpiration. The rate of transpiration is usually highest when there is a gentle breeze moving over the _____ .

    leaves/plants

126   43. Thus, one would expect a plant to transpire (more, less) when   *less*
the air is still than when the air movement is a few miles per
hour.

Contrary to what you might expect, plants also transpire less
when it is very windy because the pores in the leaves that
regulate air-exchange begin to close.

Individual Water Requirements

44. Plants differ as to their need for water. Some need to be
watered frequently. Others, like cactus, seldom need to be
_____.   *watered*

45. All plants (should, should not) be watered the same.   *should not*

46. Some plants, like jade plant and string of hearts, need to be
kept on the dry side. This means that when they are watered,
they should be watered thoroughly and then not again until
the soil almost reaches the permanent wilting point.

Jade plant

String of hearts

Creeping fig

Creeping fig, however, would probably die if watered this way. It needs to be watered long before the soil reaches the
_____ _____ _____.

permanent wilting point

47. Most plants grow more rapidly at certain times of the year and are rather dormant at others.

    Plants that are growing rapidly will need to be watered _____ often than plants that are growing _____ or are dormant.

    more
    slowly

48. Because plants have individual _____ , they (require, do not require) the same amount of water.

    needs/require-ments
    do not require

49. When a plant is growing fast, it will require_____ frequent watering than when it is growing _____.

    more
    slowly

50. You have been learning about the factors influencing the _____ of plants.

    watering

    Familiarity with these factors will help you determine _____ and _____ to water plants.

    when, how

51. The kind of container or pot in which a plant is growing affects the frequency of watering. Plants growing in clay pots need to be watered (more, less) often because the pot is _____and it loses (more, less) water vapor.

    more
    porous, more

    Plants that are growing in non-porous containers made of _____ , _____ or_____ need to be watered (more, less) often because the container loses (more, less) water vapor.

    glass, metal,
    plastic, less
    less

52. The size of the plant relative to size of the container also affects watering.

    A small plant growing in too large a container is said to be _____.

    overpotted

    A large plant growing in too small a container is said to be _____.

    underpotted

    Underpotted plants tend to get (too much, not enough) water.

    not enough

    Overpotted plants tend to be (over, under) watered and they would probably survive longer in a _____ pot.

    over
    clay/porous

53. The three basic types of soil are called_____ , _____ , and_____ . They are classified by

    sand
    clay, loam

127

the proportion of various _____ _____ *mineral particles*
they contain.

Clay soils drain (well, poorly) but they hold (much, little) *poorly, much*
water.

Clay sometimes_____when it dries out. Sandy soils *shrinks*
drain (well, poorly) and they hold (much, little) water. Loam *well, little*
soils drain (well, poorly) but they also hold quite a lot of *well*
water.

Heavy field soils are not suitable for growing potted plants
because the soil tends to stay too (wet, dry) around the roots. *wet*
Drainage can be improved by adding (finer, coarser) inorganic *coarser*
particles to the soil, such as _____ or *sand*
_____. *perlite*

Available moisture is the amount of water in the soil between
the_____ _____ and the_____ *field capacity,*
_____ _____. *permanent*
    wilting point

Clay soils have (greater, less) available moisture than do sandy *greater*
soils.

54. Environmental factors influence the frequency of watering by
their effect on transpiration rates.

Plants transpire (slower, faster) when it is warm than when it is *faster*
cool. They transpire (slower, faster) on overcast days than on *slower*
sunny days. Therefore, you would expect to water plants
growing in a north window_____ frequently than *less*
plants in a south window.

The amount of moisture in the air compared with the maximum amount of moisture the air could hold is called the
_____ _____. You would expect plants *relative humidity*
to transpire (slower, faster) when the relative humidity of their *faster*
environment is low.

Air movement also affects transpiration. The rate of transpira-
tion is highest
A. when the air is still
B. when there is a gentle breeze
C. when it is very windy *B.*

55. Plants have individual water requirements and (should, should
not) be watered the same. Jade plant and string of hearts need *should not*
to be kept on the _____ side. Creeping fig needs to *dry*
be watered_____. *frequently*

Plants require less frequent watering when they are growing
_____ or at times of the year when they are rather *slowly*
_____. *dormant*

56. Plants should be watered only when they need it. How to determine _____ a plant needs watering is easier than most people think. Several different methods can be used.

when

57. One common method is to examine the soil about half an inch below the surface. If the soil is dry, it needs _____.

water

58. Often the color of the soil surface is of some help. In general, the soil surface is darker in color when it is moist, and lighter in color when it is dry.

Therefore, if the color of the soil surface is rather dark, it may indicate that the soil is _____.

wet/moist

59. If the color of the soil surface is relatively light in color, it is an indication that the soil surface is dry, but this does not necessarily mean that the soil needs to be watered. This is because the soil a half inch below the surface may still be _____.

moist/wet

60. You may be able to tell when plants are approaching the time when they need to be watered by observing how much the soil mass has shrunk away from the sides of the pot.

This method would only be useful if the soil mix contained some _____ soil.

clay

61. Another method of telling when plants need water is to feel the leaves.

Leaves that are firm and turgid are filled with water.

A plant that has gone too long without water will feel _____.

limp/soft/ wilted/flabby

62. If, however, the leaves are not firm or _____, but not really wilted, this is an ideal time to add _____ to the soil.

turgid
water

63. If the plant were not watered at this time, it would soon
_____ .   *wilt*

64. Wilting may be another method of determining when a plant
needs to be watered. It is a severe method, however, and
sometimes is misinterpreted. Some plants wilt because they
have been overwatered long enough for the roots to rot off.
This method of determining when a plant needs to be watered
is only useful when plants are being watered correctly—leaves
of such plants will become turgid after watering. If allowed to
wilt, some plants will not recover.

If you wait until a plant _____ before watering, the   *wilts*
plant may _____ .   *die/have been*
                                                                                                     overwatered

65. Other plants that are allowed to dry out and wilt may not
_____ , but may recover partially or completely.   *die*

66. Those plants that recover only partially may lose or drop their
lower leaves but retain their _____ leaves.   *upper*

67. Although these plants recover, they are not as
_____ as healthy green plants for room decoration.   *attractive*

68. If you have been watering a plant only "when it needs it" and
it wilts, it is desperately in need of _____ .   *water/watering*

69. In general, if you wait until a plant wilts before watering it,
you are _____ too long.   *waiting*

70. Another _____ of telling when plants need _____ is to lift the pot and feel the _____ . If you do this just after watering, the pot will feel _____ . Several days later, it should feel _____ .

method
watering
weight
heavy
lighter/light

71. What at first appears to be a drastic method of determining when a plant needs to be watered is to remove the soil mass from the pot and actually inspect it. This is really a good method to use for the beginner.

The plant can be removed by spreading your left hand over the soil surface. When the rim of the pot is gently tapped against the edge of a table, the plant and soil ball should fall into your hand. After inspecting the soil, simply place the plant back into its pot. This will not harm the plant.

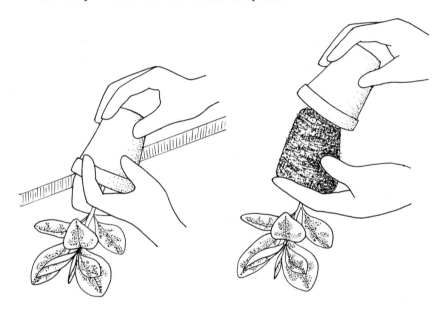

72. You should realize, however, that this method may not work if (select the one best answer):
    A. You recently potted the plant up.
    B. The soil is sandy or loose.
    C. The top of the container is narrower than the bottom.
    D. The plant is large.
    E. All of the above.

E.

73. A rather poor method of telling when a plant needs to be watered is by time. Many individuals water their plants on set schedules (so many times a week, everyday, etc.).

This method of watering is poor because it doesn't take into account such things as transpiration rates, individual _____ , and whether the plants are growing rapidly or _____ .

differences
slowly

132

74. As an additional or supplemental method of telling when plants need to be watered, the length of time that has elapsed since the last watering can be helpful.

   For example, if you check the soil and are unsure if the plant really needs to be _____ , you might recall when the plant was last watered.   *watered*

75. If the plant had been watered the day before, chances are that it doesn't need to be watered. However, if the plant hasn't been watered for a week, the probability that the soil needs to be watered is much _____ so you should probably go ahead and water it.   *greater*

76. If you water all plants on a set time schedule, you are probably always overwatering some plants and _____ others.   *underwatering*

77. Another method is to stick a toothpick into the soil. If soil particles adhere to the toothpick, then the soil is _____ .   *moist/wet*

78. Most plant growers use *several* of these methods to determine when plants need to be watered and do not rely on only _____ .   *one*

79. Water each plant _____ . Plants should be checked daily on an _____ basis. You should not water all your plants just because one of them needs _____ , since plants have individual _____ .   *when it needs it* *individual* *watering* *differences*

80. There are many different methods used for determining when plants need to be watered. The most common acceptable methods include _____ the soil, looking at the soil _____ , checking the _____ shrinkage, feeling the leaves, and carefully removing the soil and roots from the _____ .   *feeling/touching* *color, soil* *pot/container*

METHODS OF WATERING

81. The most important rule in watering plants is to water them thoroughly when they need it.

   This means that you should add enough water to the soil so that the entire soil mass becomes moist and some water drains out the bottom of the container.

   In other words, you should restore the moisture level in the soil to the _____ _____ , the level it would be after a good rain. Thorough watering (when some excess water drains out the bottom of the container) also helps prevent the buildup of excess soluble salts.   *field capacity*

82. To water thoroughly does not mean to add a thimbleful or so of water to a plant every day of the week.

    Thorough watering means to saturate the soil with water so that the entire _____ mass becomes moist, and then *soil* not to water again until the amount of moisture in the soil approaches (not reaches) the permanent wilting point.

83. A good watering schedule would look like (A, B) below.   *A*

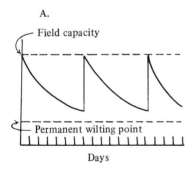

A.
┌ Field capacity
Permanent wilting point
Days

B.
┌ Field capacity
Permanent wilting point
Days

84. There are two basic ways of watering plants: from above and from below.

    The most popular and common method is to water plants from above.

    To water from above, add water to the top of the soil in the pot and allow the water to drain down (due to the pull of _____).   *gravity*

85. When you water from below, water rises due to *capillarity*. That is, the molecules of water are attracted by the solid (soil) they touch and they rise (capillary attraction) by a surface tension phenomenon.

    When you water a plant from below, the water rises because:
    A. It is pulled up by the plant.
    B. Of capillary attraction.   *B.*

86. If you water from below, you can speed up the time it takes for the water to reach the soil surface by two ways. One way is to place the pot in deep water.

    In this example, water will reach the soil surface at the top of the pot most quickly in (A, B) because of the increased water _____.

    B pressure

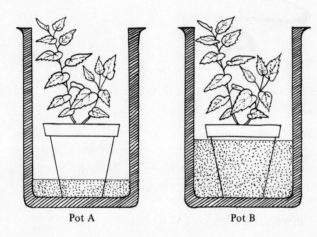

Pot A   Pot B

87. Another way to reduce the time it takes for the water to rise to the top of the soil is to use warm water.

    This is due to the fact that the molecules of warm water move (faster, slower) than molecules of cool water.   *faster*

88. Using warm water also provides more moisture for the air, which results in an increase in the relative _____.   *humidity*

89. The use of warm water will also prevent the chilling of the roots.

    This could be quite important if you have a lot of tropical houseplants which normally are from climates where the air and soil temperatures are rather (warm, cool).   *warm*

90. Some individuals water their plants from below because it is very easy to tell when the soil is thoroughly moist. All you have to do is keep adding water from below until the surface of the soil becomes _____.   *wet/moist*

91. After the entire soil mass has become saturated the excess water is allowed to drain down and out the bottom of the pot.

   After the excess water has been removed, the soil in the container will be at the (field capacity, permanent wilting point).

   field capacity

92. Another method of watering from below involves the use of a wick which runs from a water reservoir or saucer below the pot up into the soil mass in the pot.

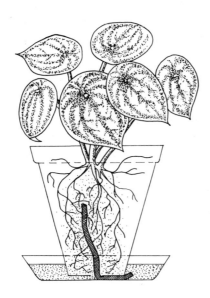

   Although this method works reasonably well for some plants sometimes, it is usually not recommended.

   Possible reasons why this type of automatic watering isn't recommended include:
   A. It doesn't take into account individual differences of plants.
   B. It doesn't take into account the environmental conditions.
   C. It doesn't take into account the type of pot, size of pot, size of plant, etc.
   D. It doesn't take into account whether a plant is growing rapidly or slowly.
   E. All of the above.

   E.

93. Having the correct soil level in a pot is helpful in insuring that a plant is watered correctly. The correct soil level is ½ to 1 inch or more from the top of the pot, depending on the size of the pot.

   All pots (should, should not) be filled to the same level with soil.

   should not

94. This space at the top of the pot serves as a reservoir. It should be large enough to hold sufficient water so that the soil in the pot can be thoroughly moistened with only one filling.

The pot filled to the correct level is (A, B, C).   *C*

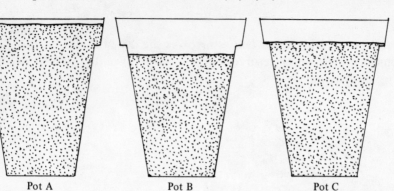

Pot A   Pot B   Pot C

95. Sometimes, however, you have to add water several times at one watering regardless of the soil level. This occurs when the soil mass shrinks sufficiently so that there is a space between the soil and the pot. The water runs through this space and out the bottom of the pot without wetting the whole soil mass.

This could happen quite often if there were a lot of _____ in the soil mix.   *clay*

96. What you need to do if there is a large amount of clay in the soil is to add small amounts of water several different times at intervals of a few minutes.

    If water runs out the bottom of a container, you (can, cannot) always be sure that the entire soil mass is moist.   *cannot*

97. After the soil swells up enough to come into contact with the pot all the way around, then you can fill the reservoir with water as you would normally do.

    A sandy soil will probably take (more, less) time to water than a clay soil.   *less*

98. Having the correct soil level is important whether you water from the top or from the bottom. This is because it is best to water from the top once every few weeks even though you normally water from the bottom.

    It is best to have an adequate reservoir at the top of a pot even though you normally water from the _____.   *bottom*

99. The reason for watering from the top occasionally is to flush the minerals and salts that accumulate at the soil surface down through the soil and out the bottom of the pot—a process called leaching.

    Water contains minerals and salts which tend to accumulate at the soil _____ when plants are watered from below.   *surface*

100. A white crust of minerals and salts usually builds up on the surface of the soil even if you do flush the soil out periodically. If the crust is unsightly, you might skim it off carefully without disturbing the root system, or you might want to cover it up with some pebbles or other materials.

    The white crust on soil comes mainly from the minerals and salts in the (soil, water), or from overfertilization.   *water*

101. When watering plants, you should avoid getting water on the leaves (except for an occasional shower to remove dust), because the _____ _____ will streak or spot the leaves.   *mineral deposits*

102. If you have a choice of water to use, select the purest water possible.

    Water containing large amounts of minerals and salts will spot the foliage and build up the soil to such high levels that some essential mineral elements become tied up in the soil. The result is that some essential mineral elements are no longer available to the plant.

If a plant has been growing in the same soil for a long time (especially in a planter or dish garden that has no drainage hole), the salts may build up to a point where the plant ceases to grow, or may even begin to die. The plant may be helped by repotting it in fresh soil.

Plants growing in planters or dish gardens with no drainage holes may live longer if they are watered with _____ water.   *pure/distilled*

103. Rain water and distilled water would probably be the two _____ types of water readily available.   *purest*

104. If you don't have access to rain or distilled water, then you should use well water if available. Next best would be unsoftened tap water and lastly, softened tap water.

If you wanted your plants to last a long time, particularly those that are permanently grown in small containers holding little soil, you would not want to use _____ water.   *softened tap*

105. So far in our discussion of watering we have assumed that the containers had drainage holes in the bottom.

Plants are easiest to care for in this type of container because excess water can always drain out the bottom of the pot.

You will probably have more success in growing houseplants if you use containers that have _____ .   *drainage holes*

106. Occasionally a clay pot containing a plant is placed inside a slightly larger ornamental pot that doesn't have drainage holes.

By using this procedure, you are able to combine the benefits of having drainage holes in the container in which the plant is actually growing with the benefit of having the plant appearing in an _____ container.

ornamental/ attractive

107. This larger, outside ornamental pot is often referred to as a *jardiniere* (jar di NIERE)—an ornamental pot or stand for flowers or plants.

Such jardinieres are glazed so that moisture doesn't seep through them onto the surface beneath.

Clay saucers which can be purchased for clay pots should not be used on good surfaces such as wooden tables because the saucers allow moisture to pass through due to their being very _____ .

porous

108. In case plants are actually grown in containers which lack drainage holes, then watering will be (more, less) of a problem.

more

109. Drainage in this type of container is sometimes provided by placing a shallow layer of gravel, broken crockery, charcoal, or other similar material in the bottom of the pot.

This is a safety precaution in case you should mistakenly (underwater, overwater) your plants.

overwater

110. This drainage layer also provides a place for the excess drainage water which is bound to appear if you water plants _____ as you are supposed to do. (However, capillarity will cause this water to rise, so try not to overwater.)

thoroughly

111. Early morning is the most popular time for watering plants in greenhouses.

In the home, the time of day for watering plants isn't as critical unless you get water on the foliage.

The time of day when plants are watered (may be, may not be) important.

may be

112. Time of watering is important because leaves that are wet for many hours at a time are much more susceptible to attack by diseases.

Since prevention of diseases is easier than curing them, greenhouse operators find it smart to water early enough in the day to insure that the plants will be dried off by evening. Greenhouse operators almost never water plants at (noon, 5 P.M.)

5 P.M.

140

113. It would be well to follow the greenhouse operator's practice of not watering late in the day if:
    A. Plants are crowded.
    B. You have to get water on the foliage when you water.
    C. The humidity is high.
    D. All of the above.   *D.*

114. Plants can either be watered from _____ or from   *above*
    _____ .   *below*

    Whichever method is used, plants should be watered
    _____ and then not watered again until they   *thoroughly*
    _____ it.   *need*

    When you water from above, water drains down due to the
    pull of_____. When you water from below, the   *gravity*
    water rises due to _____ _____ . When   *capillary*
    watering from below, you can speed up the time it takes for   *attraction*
    the water to reach the soil surface by placing the pot in
    _____ water or by using _____ water.   *deep, warm*

115. Having the correct soil level in a pot is helpful for insuring that
    a plant is watered correctly. The space at the top of the pot
    serves as a _____ and it should hold sufficient water   *reservoir*
    to thoroughly moisten all the soil in the pot with one
    watering.

References

Abraham, George. *The Green Thumb Book of Indoor Gardening: A Complete Guide.* Englewood Cliffs, N.J.: Prentice-Hall, 1967. 304 pp.

Ballard, Ernesta D. *Growing Plants Indoors: A Garden in Your House.* New York: Barnes & Noble Books (Harper & Row), 1973. 258 pp.

Beatty, Virginia L., and the Editors of Consumer Guide. *Consumer Guide Rating and Raising Indoor Plants: A Practical Guide for Successful Indoor Gardening.* Skokie, Ill.: Publications International, 1975. 352 pp.

Free, Montague. *All about House Plants.* Garden City, N.Y.: The American Garden Guild and Doubleday & Co., 1946. 328 pp.

Graf, Alfred B. *Exotica Series Three.* 8th ed. East Rutherford, N.J.: Roehrs, 1976.

————. *Exotic Plant Manual: Exotic Plants to Live With.* 4th ed. East Rutherford, N.J.: Roehrs, 1976.

Hersey, Jean D. *Woman's Day Book of House Plants.* New York: Simon & Schuster, 1965. 128 pp.

Herwig, Rob, and Margot Schubert. *The Treasury of Houseplants.* New York: Macmillan Co., 1976. 368 pp.

Huxley, Anthony. *House Plants, Cacti, and Succulents.* London: Hamlyn Publishing Co., 1973. 133 pp.

Kromdijk, G. *Two-Hundred House Plants in Color.* Translated by A. M. H. Speller. New York: Herder & Herder, 1973. 224 pp.

McDonald, Elvin. *The World Book of House Plants.* Cleveland: World Publishing Co., 1963. 318 pp.

Nicolaisen, Age. *Pocket Encyclopedia of Indoor Plants in Color.* Edited by Richard Goren. New York: Macmillan Co., 1970. 269 pp.

Rochford, Thomas, and Richard Gorer. *Rochford's Book of House-Plants.* London: Faber & Faber, 1971. 240 pp.

Glossary

ACCLIMATIZATION: Preparing foliage plants gradually for a change in environment, usually from a protected place such as a greenhouse, where growing conditions are at optimum levels, to a rather severe environment like a home, where the air is dry and the light intensity is low. Similar to hardening off.

ADVENTITIOUS: A term used to classify roots and other plant parts according to origin. Adventitious roots are roots that grow out of a structure other than a primary or secondary root, such as a stem.

ANNUAL: An herbaceous plant that lives for only one growing season, produces flowers, and dies. Marigold and zinnia are examples.

APICAL DOMINANCE: The inhibiting effect of the apical, or terminal, bud over the lateral, or axillary, buds beneath it.

ARTIFICIAL SOIL MIX: A soil or growing mix (medium) made up entirely of peat moss, vermiculite or perlite, and fertilizers, without any loam or field soil. Leaf mold and bark are other materials used in artificial soil mixes.

AUXINS: Plant hormones such as indoleacetic acid, indolebutyric acid, and napthalencacetic acid which are used as rooting hormones, herbicides, and defoliants.

AVAILABLE MOISTURE: The amount of moisture in soil between the field capacity and the permanent wilting point.

AXILLARY BUD: The bud in the axil of a leaf, a lateral bud.

BEDDING PLANTS: Plants used in masses (beds) for showy and striking effects. Common bedding plants include petunia, zinnia, marigold, begonia, geranium, snapdragon, and sweet alyssum, as well as many others.

BIENNIAL: A plant that lives for 2 years or parts of 2 years. Biennial plants grow vegetatively the first year and flower the second year. Some biennial plants, such as snapdragons and pansies, are treated as annuals and are sold in the spring of the year that they will flower.

BIGENERIC HYBRID: A hybrid whose parents belong to different genera. Fatshedera is a cross between *Fatsia japonica* and *Hedera helix*.

BINOMIAL: The scientific name of a plant or animal. It is composed of two (bi) parts, the genus and the species. The scientific name of poinsettia is *Euphorbia pulcherrima; Euphorbia* is the genus and *pulcherrima* the species.

BOTANY: The plant science that is concerned with the study of non-cultivated (wild) plants.

BROMELIAD: A plant belonging to the Bromeliaceae, or pineapple family.

BULBS: In general, this term refers both to plants that reproduce by underground structures such as corms and tubers, and to true bulbs like tulip, hyacinth, and daffodil. A true bulb consists of a small stem at its lower end, with many fleshy, scale-like leaves growing from the upper surface of the stem (e.g., onion, lily, tulip).

CAMBIUM: The layer of meristematic cells between the xylem and phloem tissues in stems, roots, and rhizomes.

CAPILLARITY: The attraction of molecules of water by a solid such as soil or growing medium. Water rises in a pot of soil because of capillarity.

COMMON NAME: The name or names by which plants, animals, and insects are known, for example, pine, oak, coleus, horse, ladybug. Often more than one common name is used around the country and the world for the same plant or animal.

COMPLETE FERTILIZER: A fertilizer that contains all three major elements—nitrogen, phosphorus, and potassium.

CORTEX: The tissues in a stem or root that lie between the epidermis and the endodermis.

COTYLEDON: The part of the embryo that stores and digests food. Seeds of monocots have one cotyledon or seed leaf; seeds of dicots have two cotyledons.

CULTIVAR: A cultivated variety. Cultivars are nearly always maintained by vegetative propagation.

CUTTING: Any vegetative part of a plant which is capable of regenerating the missing plant parts when removed from the parent.

DESICCATION: The drying up of leaves and stems. It often occurs after transplanting if plants are not protected from wind and sunlight. New cuttings also need protection until they root. Covering cuttings with a plastic bag is one way of increasing humidity and will help to prevent desiccation.

DORMANCY: A period of rest, caused by internal conditions, which occurs in many seeds before they will germinate.

DOUBLE-POTTING: Placing one pot inside a larger pot and perhaps filling the space between the two pots with a moisture-holding material such as sphagnum moss, peat moss, or vermiculite.

ENDODERMIS: A layer of cells inside the cortex and adjacent to the pericycle.

ESSENTIAL ELEMENT: An element present in soil or air that is necessary for normal plant growth and development, either as a component of the plant's structure or as a requirement for physiological processes.

ETIOLATION: The excessive stem elongation (long internodes) found in plants grown under low light intensity. Etiolated plants appear tall and spindly.

FERTILIZATION: The union of egg and sperm.

FERTILIZER: A material added to soils or growing media to provide nutrients for plant growth.

FIELD CAPACITY: The amount of water present in soil or growing medium after a thorough rain or watering.

FLOWER: The characteristic reproductive structure of angiosperms. Most flowers bear four kinds of floral organs: sepals, petals, stamens, and pistil.

FORCING: The process of bringing plants, branches, and bulbs into flower ahead of their normal outdoor flowering period.

FRUIT: A matured ovary or cluster of matured ovaries. Each ovary may contain one or more seeds. Fruits are the containers that seeds come in.

GARBAGE-CAN HORTICULTURE: Using commonly discarded plants or plant parts as a basis for inexpensive plant projects. Examples include rooting a pineapple top, growing an avocado from the pit, and digging up and repotting such bedding plants as wax begonias and coleus in the fall before a frost.

GENUS: The taxonomic unit between family and species. A genus includes one or more species.

GEOTROPISM: A hormone-regulated response of stems and roots to gravity.

GERMINATION: The sprouting of a seed or spore.

GRAFTING: A method of vegetative propagation in which parts of two different plants are joined together in such a way that they unite and grow as a single plant.

GROWING MEDIUM: The medium or soil mixture in which plants are grown. Mixtures used for growing many indoor plants are: peat moss and vermiculite; peat moss and perlite; peat moss, loam, and sand or perlite; peat moss, leaf mold, loam, and sand or perlite; and other similar growing media.

HARDENING OFF: Preparing plants gradually for a change in environment, usually from a protected environment such as a greenhouse, where growing conditions are at optimum levels, to a rather severe environment like a garden, where the plants will have to get along on their own. For vegetables and bedding plants, the process usually involves one or more of the following: lowering the humidity, increasing the air circulation, reducing the frequency of watering and fertilizing, and subjecting the plants to greater extremes of temperature. The same principles also apply to the transfer of houseplants from one environment to another (greenhouse to home). Houseplants should also be subjected to lower light intensities to slow down their rate of growth and to help prepare them for the low light conditions of most homes. When applied to foliage plants, this process is also known as acclimatization.

HARDINESS: The degree to which plants can withstand subfreezing temperatures. Hardy plants and bulbs, like peonies and tulips, can tolerate subfreezing temperatures outdoors in winter. Tender plants and bulbs cannot withstand subfreezing temperatures.

HARDY: This term applies to plants that can survive subfreezing temperatures.

HERBACEOUS PERENNIAL: A perennial plant, such as a peony, that has green herbaceous stems that die back to the ground at the end of each growing season. Only the root system remains alive.

HERBS: Plants which do not develop much woody tissue and which usually have rather succulent annual stems. This term also refers to a much smaller group of plants (chives, dill, sage, etc.) grown for seasoning foods.

HILUM: The scar on a seed coat where the seed stalk was attached to the seed.

HORTICULTURE: The area of agriculture that includes fruits, vegetables, trees, shrubs, turf, ground covers, flowers, and small ornamental plants. Horticulture is both an art and a science.

LEACHING: The process of flushing accumulated minerals and salts out of soil or growing media by adding enough water to the surface so that a considerable amount drains out the bottom of the container. Plants watered from below need to be leached more frequently than plants watered from above, since some leaching will occur each time the plant is watered thoroughly from above.

MERISTEM: A mass of growing cells found at stem and root tips. These cells are capable of frequent cell division.

MICROPYLE: The minute opening in a seed through which the pollen tube grew prior to fertilization.

NON-VEGETATIVE (SEXUAL) PROPAGATION: Propagation involving the union of egg and sperm and the formation of seeds.

PEAT MOSS: A propagating material composed of partially decomposed plants. It usually is used in combination with sand or perlite because of its high water-holding capacity and poor aeration.

PERENNIAL: A plant that lives several to many years, producing both leaves and flowers each growing season after it has reached maturity.

PERICYCLE: A layer of cells in stems and roots, between the endodermis and the phloem. Branch roots arise from this layer.

PERLITE: A propagation material made from volcanic rock (lava). It is very light and porous.

PERMANENT WILTING POINT: The amount of water left in the soil or growing medium when a plant wilts and can't recover.

pH: A symbol for a scale that indicates acidity or alkalinity. A pH of 7 is neutral. A very acid soil has a pH of 4 to 5. A pH of 8 and above is very alkaline. Almost all plants require a pH somewhere between 4 and 8, with the majority doing best between a pH of 6.5 and 7.0 (slightly acid to neutral). Most houseplants grow best in slightly to moderately acid soil, 5.5 to 6.8. The acidity of soil is affected by the water and fertilizers used. An occasional soil test may be beneficial if you are having plant problems or are growing plants on a large scale. Acid-loving houseplants include ferns and cyclamen, whereas cast-iron plant, chlorophytum, and cyperus grow best in soil that is neutral to slightly alkaline.

PHLOEM: A conducting tissue in plants, the chief function of which is food conduction downward.

PHOTOTROPISM: A growth movement or bending due to the stimulus of light.

PINCHING: Removal of the growing tip (terminal bud) of a plant in order to allow the axillary (lateral) buds to grow. The result is a more bushy, compact plant. Only plants having conspicuous upright stems need be pinched.

PITH: The tissue in the center of a stem.

PLANT GROWTH REGULATORS: The "chemical messengers" which affect plant growth and development. They include both natural chemical messengers (hormones) and commercially available synthetic materials.

POLLINATION: The transfer of pollen from the anther of a stamen to a stigma.

PROPAGATING MEDIUM: The medium or soil mix used for rooting cuttings or starting seeds. Common propagating media include coarse sand, vermiculite, perlite, and mixtures of vermiculite or perlite with peat moss.

RELATIVE HUMIDITY: The amount of moisture in the air compared with the maximum amount of moisture that the air could hold. Warm air can hold much more moisture than cold air. The relative humidity of air, therefore, decreases when it is heated.

REPOTTING: Transferring a plant into the next larger size pot when it outgrows the one that it is in.

SCARIFICATION: Any process which overcomes physical dormancy of seeds by altering the seed coat. Scratching or breaking the seed coat and soaking seeds in hot water or acid are common methods.

SCIENTIFIC NAME: A name consisting of *two parts,* the first being the name of the genus and the second the name of the species. All plants and animals have only *one* scientific name; for example, *Mimosa pudica* is the common "sensitive plant."

SCION: The top part of a graft.

SEED: The characteristic reproductive structure of seed plants; a mature ovule.

SORUS: A cluster of sporangia on a fern frond. Plural is sori.

SPECIES: The smallest natural unit to which a plant belongs. Taxonomically it ranks below genus but above subspecies and cultivar.

SPHAGNUM MOSS: A propagating medium composed of the remains of bog plants. It is used especially for seed germination because it contains fungi-statics which help suppress damping-off diseases.

SPORE: An asexual reproductive structure of many plants such as ferns, mosses, algae, and fungi.

STOCK: The lower part of a graft, also called the understock or rootstock.

STRATIFICATION: A seed treatment that involves storing seeds under cool and moist conditions (about $40°F$ for 1 to 4 months) to overcome physiological dormancy (dormancy as a result of seed-coat effects).

SUCCULENT: Any plant that has the ability to store moisture in thick, fleshy stems or leaves. Succulents occur in many different plant families and include aloe, bryophyllum, cacti, crown-of-thorns, jade plant, jelly beans, peperomias, snake plant, string of hearts, wax plant, and many others. Most succulents make excellent houseplants if not overwatered.

TENDER: A term used to describe plants that are not hardy (cannot withstand subfreezing temperatures).

TRANSPLANTING: Moving plants from one location to another—from one pot to another, usually larger, pot (repotting)—and seedlings from a seedbed or flat to a pot (potting or potting up).

TROPISM: The bending of a plant part as a result of differences in growth rate induced by external stimuli.

VEGETATIVE (ASEXUAL) PROPAGATION: Propagation from vegetative portions of a plant, such as stem and root cuttings, tubers, grafts, spores, separation, and so on.

VERMICULITE: A material derived from the mineral mica and used in propagating plants. It is very light in weight and can absorb a lot of water.

VIABILITY: The ability to live and grow.

XYLEM: A conducting tissue in plants through which water and minerals move upward. Xylem makes up the major portion of wood in a tree.

Index

Weeds, 42
Whip-and-tongue graft, 69
Whiteflies, 41
Whole-leaf cutting, 67-68
Wilting, 129, 130
    See also Permanent wilting point
Wounding, 73

Xylem, 3, 6, 10

Zebra plant, 77